FORGED AS ONE

One Lord, One Faith, One Glorious Hope

Ricky Smith

Edited by Readable Reach, readablereach.com

**Readable
Reach**

Cover design by Laura Atterbury, Calvary Baptist Church

All Scripture references are from the English Standard Version of the Holy Bible.

Forged As One: One Lord, One Faith, One Glorious Hope

ISBN: 978-1-7359462-0-7

This book is dedicated to the wonderful faith family of Calvary Baptist Church in Columbus, Georgia, who forged together in unity while navigating the unprecedented pandemic of 2020.

Behold, how good and pleasant it is when brothers dwell in unity!
—PSALM 133:1 ESV

CONTENTS

INTRODUCTION

As you scan the landscape of American culture today, there is strong evidence that we have a fractured society that has lost the ability to discuss, reason, agree, and work together. Sadly, for many churches, we are a microcosm of this same level of division within our local fellowships.

The world will never live in unity if even the church cannot demonstrate unity.

Jesus prayed that we (believers) may be one as He and the Father are one (John 17:21). Unity in the Church is absolutely essential to complete the mission we have been given, namely to spread the good news of the Gospel to the world. For us to live as one, this implies a common goal, a shared mission and submitted hearts.

But, many things hinder the Church from being fully unified. We are sinners, and our sin and weakness gets in the way. Often the debates and arguments inside our churches are over topics that have little to no impact on the Gospel. We love to debate on the color of the carpet, the intensity of the lights and the financial report. Truthfully, these are signs of individuals who are focused on themselves rather than being fully submitted to the Lordship of Christ.

However, Jesus is the great unifier. In Him we live, move, and have our being, as the Bible says in Acts 17. If we get to know Him more and keep our eyes focused on Him, we can together make an impact on the eternity of those around us, and a greater impact than we could make alone. In Him and through Him we can rise to the challenge and provide leadership and vision that our culture desperately needs.

In this book, I use the language of being *forged* on purpose. Forging implies a tighter, stronger unity than we would normally think of when we hear the word *unity*. I want to see the Church truly bonded and focused on the same goal. This vision applies to a local church, a network of churches and even reaching across denominational lines.

In this book, we will use Ephesians chapter 4 as a driver. We will walk through it verse by verse to describe our calling from God, what it looks like to be unified, what keeps us from true unity, and how to work our spiritual muscles to grow more into the forged Church God desires us to be.

Originally this began as an exegetical sermon series, and it has now been cultivated into a tool for personal or group study.

Unity is not easy, but when we see glimmers of it, it is beautiful, and it honors our Lord. Picking up this book is a first step toward all of us growing and maturing together into a forged body of believers that will grow God's Kingdom. Imagine the impact that could be witnessed if the people of God lived and acted as a forged unit of love and with a commitment to carry hope to the world!

Chapter One

UNITED TOGETHER

A hammer has a lot of power, because it has been *forged* together. The forging gives it incredible strength. However, if you were to separate the atoms that make up the hammer, each of them would fall like snowflakes.

But in a hammer, the atoms have been welded into one unit. They have been welded by the firm hand of the forger, and therefore, the hammer has power to obliterate a rock and break it into pieces.

The imagery of a hammer is a picture of God's design for the church and one that we'll study throughout this book. Any item that has been forged together requires pressure in order to become one unit. It also often requires heat, and it is that stress (heat and pressure) that causes it to take on new life.

The coronavirus pandemic has certainly provided stress and pressure for the Church, and I personally have observed two peaks of fear and anxiety. When it started, everybody was afraid; people were reactive. But then, we settled into the new reality. We just accepted, regardless of our opinions, the stay-at-home situation. Then, there was a wave of anxiety, maybe even stress, and differing opinions as churches began to open back up again.

When pressure like that comes, lean in, and allow us as Jesus' Church to be forged in unity through it, to be a voice of ease and hope, rather than distraction. Let's allow it to bind us, to grow us, to unite us, to forge us together, even when we are individually apart.

Identity

Ephesians 4 in the Bible will be our framework for our study on being forged in unity. As we dive in, there are a few observations I want us to make in the first few verses. In verses one and two, we see identity. We see a framework here of how God wants us to live.

Ephesians 4:1-2

I therefore, a prisoner for the Lord, urge you to walk in a manner worthy of the calling to which you have been called, with all humility and gentleness, with patience, bearing with one another in love.

This is a strong and powerful start. Paul references three things that I want to unpack. He references his identity in Christ, his walk with Christ and his calling from Christ.

Let's first think about the idea of identity. In our culture today, it is very common when we meet someone for the very first time (maybe in the grocery store or at a party, especially among men) to say, "Hey, what do you do for a living?"

In one vein, it is a desire to surface-level get to know someone, because it's a safe question. When you think about it, though, sometimes we unintentionally attach our identity to what we do, and we're prone to measure who we are based on what we do.

I think this has created, truthfully, an unhealthy identity crisis in the Church, in our culture and in the world. In fact, underneath it is this sense of pride, arrogance and ego. It's me trying to say, "Hey, am I a little more validated in what I do than what you do?" And so, it leads to fracturing rather than forging.

The Christian life calls us to live counter to what culture says is normal. We are called to live worthy of our calling (Ephesians 4:1). But what does that mean? Through my study of the original language, I learned that the text literally could be translated, "Live deservingly of the identity that you have been summoned for, or called, or crafted to be."

Think of it this way: I remember as a boy being challenged from time to time by my father to step into social situations and make wise choices that would bring honor to the family name and not disgrace it.

Or a different example that perhaps you could relate to is if you've ever been part of a sports team or a band where you went out in public as part of a group. You were always told, "Hey listen; your actions are a reflection on the team."

It pushes against this idea that I'm the only one who matters. I realize that my walk, my conduct and my life impact others. We get this culturally, but it is so much more significant when we understand that we, as God's people, literally bear and carry the name of Jesus. 1 Peter 4:16 says:

1 Peter 4:16

Yet, if anyone suffers as a Christian, let him not be ashamed, but let him glorify God in that name.

Jesus has already called my name. I am His, and we as His people, those who have put our trust in Him, have been called out of darkness into God's marvelous light (1 Peter 2:9). We are called into the grace of Christ (Galatians 1:6). We are called into the fellowship of Christ (1 Corinthians 1:9). We are called unto holiness (1 Thessalonians 2:7). We are called to be a voice of peace (1 Corinthians 7:15). Therefore, we might as well walk in a way that is consistent with the identity to which we have been summoned.

This not only causes me to shape, or reshape, my choices so that I don't bring shame on the name of Jesus, but it should call me to value His name more than my own.

As we are rearing our children, we may encourage something like, "Hey, go make a name for yourself." And, we understand what that means from a sense of setting goals, but what God says is, "Make much of *my* name; glorify *my* name." My identity as a man is forged into Him, and it brings me strength, peace and stability.

Paul understands this when he begins verse one of chapter four with, "I am a prisoner for the Lord." There is this statement of identity, of recognizing a deflection of any praise to him. But then he moves into this idea of our walk.

The Greek word used here for "to walk" suggests something different from a casual stroll. It means to follow a prescribed way in a fixed order. In fact, it's comparable to the army of Israel marching under God's guidance in the wilderness. They were following a pillar of cloud by day and pillar of fire by night, and there was a determination to set their eyes fixed on their guide, to walk under His guidance.

If I were to compare this to something we can hang a hat on, it would be this: It's not a leisurely stroll in the evening walking the dog down the road. This would actually be more akin to if I'm sent to the mall on a shopping errand for my wife. I'm not casually going to the mall; I am in and out. I have a direct mission. I have something I'm trying to accomplish. I've got my eyes fixed. I'm walking in this door. I'm even trying to navigate the most efficient path.

So, there is this determined, consistent, fixed walk. That's the idea. But it begs this question, how am I to do this? How am I to walk on this mission? Paul specifically says "worthy of the calling which you've been called."

Who talks like that? What does that mean? Well, let me put it to you this way: This is a call of conduct that is consistent over time throughout your life. Our actions should be consistent with our mission with God, paying more attention to His name and His desire than our own.

You and I have the ability to spot inconsistencies. We can pick them out quickly. If we're being honest, we are really good at quickly pointing out inconsistencies in *other* people's conduct, are we not? But we're also pretty quick to pick them out even in ourselves internally, and that may lead to some insecurities, anxiety or stress, because we know, *I'm not doing what I should do. I'm not living the way that I should live.*

Later in Ephesians 4, Paul deals with that tension very specifically. For now, I want us to focus on the desire, the ideal of this walk being consistent and on mission with God. This means that my interaction with my neighbor, my relationship with my wife, my interaction and the quality of my experience with my co-workers will be shaped by my walk. So, live *worthy*, not just morally right.

Anybody can talk about the value of making good moral choices. That's not what we're talking about. We're talking about living worthy of the calling that God has placed on our life. God has called us to live under His name. God has called us to live under His influence. And living under His authority results in the fruit of the Spirit of God being on display. It gains strength and impact when we walk worthy of the calling. So, we need to pay attention to what that calling is.

The Calling of Christ

Let me offer three suggestions on how this calling in Christ could be described. This is not my description; it comes from three different unique passages of Scripture.

1. High

The first is that it is a high calling. We read this in Philippians:

Philippians 3:14

I press on toward the goal for the prize of the upward call of God in Christ Jesus

Some of your translations may say, "High calling of God in Christ Jesus." There is this high calling, to which a prize is attached for eternal life. You have a calling that comes from on high, and it calls you to soar to new heights. The language in the New Testament is one of striving, being eager, to press for, to pursue. The challenge is to reach deeper into an understanding of God and His Word, and then to soar and fly above, mounted up on wings like eagles (Isaiah 40:31), above our fear as we trust in Christ and in His plan.

He has a high calling. His desire is not for us to be lowly and defeated, but to be victorious and conquerors.

2. Holy

It is also a Holy calling. 2 Timothy 1:8 and 9 says:

> *2 Timothy 1:8-9*
>
> *Therefore do not be ashamed of the testimony about our Lord, nor of me his prisoner, but share in suffering for the gospel by the power of God, who saved us and called us to a holy calling, not because of our works but because of his own purpose and grace, which he gave us in Christ Jesus before the ages began.*

There is a whole chapter we could write about that passage alone, but what I want us to understand is, God's purpose for us is to pursue Him with holiness. My calling is not because of my goodness, but because of His grace. And here we see the Gospel at work where His righteousness has been given to me. This is the really strong theological word *imputation*. I have been declared righteous, justified in Him.

I have been made right in His sight. I have been imputed with His righteousness, and therefore, as I work that out in my salvation, I grow with a desire toward this Holy calling, to think His thoughts and be like Him.

The very nature of discipleship in the New Testament is that the disciple becomes just like his teacher. As I begin to work out my salvation, there is a desire to become more like Jesus.

3. Heavenly Calling

Third, the calling is heavenly. Hebrews 3:1 and 2 says:

> *Hebrews 3:1-2*
>
> *Therefore, holy brothers, you who share in a heavenly calling, consider Jesus, the apostle and high priest of our confession, who was faithful to him who appointed him, just as Moses also was faithful in all God's house.*

This world is not my home. I am not a citizen of here. I am a citizen of Heaven. That is where my citizenship lies as a child of God. I am an alien (some translations say a foreigner) here on this Earth. I shouldn't fit in.

Let's use a bit of logic around the idea of a *call*. Since we are talking about a *calling*, there must be a *caller*. But, who is the one making the call? Does it make a difference who calls? I think it does. Think about it this way: If you are sitting in your house and your sibling calls your name, you blow it off, right? But, if your mom or dad calls your name (especially if they throw the middle name in there with it), you pay attention. There is a striking difference in how we respond based on who calls us.

So, here we see that there is a calling, which implies there is a caller, and the caller is God Himself. When Jesus calls my name, I am going to listen and pay attention. Remember that this call comes from above, from the Father. The Son mediates for us to obtain it. The Holy Spirit applies it to our lives. And the reality of this calling is that it impacts every day of your life.

The context of what Paul is saying initially is remembering that my identity comes *from* Christ, and *for* Christ, and it impacts the way I walk and live. Therefore, I cannot separate my faith from my life. It truly is the core of my identity. It impacts my relationships, my choices and my future.

Thus, it impacts where the rubber meets the road. Let me illustrate. My family is working through going back and watching all the Marvel Universe movies. One of the key ingredients of that whole story is the Infinity Stones from the Avengers.[1] If you don't have any clue what this is talking about, don't worry about it.

The whole concept is that the more these stones assemble together, the more it creates this powerful force to be reckoned with. I want to use that idea, that concept, to help us see some "stones" that specifically are traits of our character that point to the name that we bear when we allow them to shine and be exposed. The more these "stones" come together, the more impact we can have in the world.

Stones of Unity

1. Humility

The first one is the stone of humility, remembering who we were when God's grace took hold of us. It means a lowliness of mind, a humble recognition of worth, and the value of other people. It is the opposite of pride. Instead, it leads us to value the grace that God has extended to us and the willingness to view others the way that He sees them.

As this stone begins to radiate and be reflected in our walk and conduct, as we respond to God's calling in life, we decrease, He increases and we begin to see others more like God sees them.

2. Gentleness

There is a stone of gentleness. In some translations, depending on what you are using, it may use the word *meekness* here. This is not the idea of being weak or passive. It is actually very active. It is power in understanding the strength that I have, but it is under control.

It is under someone else's authority. It is like a bridled beast, and practically, this works in tandem with self control. It helps us remain calm under pressure, unlike how I acted at Lowe's the other day when I had to wait in line four times to buy one thing. There was not a spirit of meekness coming out in me, I confess. My flesh began to show, and the pressure in that didn't bring the best out of me.

I simply say that as an example, that we are all working this out. Meekness or gentleness in practice will lead me to be slow to get angry.

3. Patience

The third stone here is one of patience. It is commanded by God in Romans 12:17 and is illustrated through Christ's teaching in Matthew 5:44. Ultimately, it is modeled by Christ when we read 1 Peter 2:21-23.

1 Peter 2:21-23

For to this you have been called, because Christ also suffered for you, leaving you an example, so that you might follow in his steps. He committed no sin, neither was deceit found in his mouth. When he was reviled, he did not revile in return; when he suffered, he did not threaten, but continued entrusting himself to him who judges justly.

Notice the language that brings back the imagery of this walk. What an example that Christ has modeled for you and me to be patient!

4. Love

Last we see, bearing one another in love. It is a love that covers a multitude of sins out of grace and mercy, like being expressed and described in 1 Corinthians 13. This is the trademark expression of the Christian faith that we read of in John 13:35, "This is how all men will know that you are my disciples, if you love one another."

It impacts how you love your wife. It impacts how you lead your children. It impacts how you serve your neighbor. Remember who you were and what you were when you had a call of love in your life, when the grace of God was extended to you, the Holy Spirit convicted you of your sin, and you recognized your need to submit to His authority. Remember the love that you received, and model that for others.

Maybe you were unloving. Perhaps you were unlovable. Here we see these attributes, these characteristics of our walk that should come out of someone who is identifying *with* Christ and *for* Christ. That consistent walk is by God's help and within reach of all of us.

I would say it is an impressive and continual sermon to the world. It is an unanswerable sermon to the world that you cannot argue with. In essence, it is the sermon that you and I are called to preach.

Let's all preach this sermon. Preach it in your walk, your talk, your life, your interaction and expression. It makes the world brighter and better. Your walk should display love at every step, and our walk as a collective group of believers proclaiming hope in Christ is watched, and it impacts Gospel conversations.

Our conduct affects our ability for others to understand the hope of the Gospel. Our inability to show patience and love can give people an excuse to reject our message.

Fashioned for Unity

We see from Ephesians 4:3 this idea that we are fashioned for unity.

Ephesians 4:3

Eager to maintain the unity of the Spirit in the bond of peace.

We are eager to maintain each of the stones, or markers, of our identity. They display the spirit, which bonds us together as believers. Remember, Ephesians 4:1 began with the word *therefore*. That tells you there is a lot that has been discussed in the preceding chapters that we should pay close attention to.

And I would submit to you, go back and read chapters one through three of Ephesians, where Paul has been pointing out the unsearchable and immeasurable riches of God. He has unpacked the doctrine of salvation by grace through faith in chapter two, and at numerous times, he has pointed that we are to walk together.

Here in chapter four is this huge statement, or call, to unity. This vivid reinforcement of faith reminds us that God has not designed, nor has He intended, for us to exercise faith all alone.

We are a group of people together on a mission FOR one God, one faith, one glorious hope, one baptism, but not OF one. This is not an individual mission. This is not an individual expression. It is a collective, unifying expression of hope as we carry it to the world. And God has not intended us to do this all alone.

I may walk in rhythm, singing a melody of love, but God is more glorified when we all walk in unison with the Spirit and create this beautiful masterpiece, or melody of love that sings a song of hope to Him. The enemy would love for us to live in isolation. He would love for us to live forever distanced from one another. But God has not designed us to walk that way. He has created us to walk in relationship with Him and in relationship with one another, in unity.

There were about three years of my life, professionally, where I worked as a state missionary, and I traveled all the time. I think on average, I spent 120-125 nights a year in a hotel somewhere. I was gone all the time. In all my travels across the state, across the country, I was separated from my wife and children by miles. But in our hearts, we were still unified as one.

We had to work intentionally and diligently to maintain that communication and that connectedness. We had to maintain the discipline by phone or video, praying together and having family worship together every night. It took work, but we were still together, united on mission, even if we were distant.

We as Christians may be divided by thousands of miles from the saints in Australia and the South Pacific sea, but we live as brothers and sisters in Christ, unified in the Spirit.

To give you an example, Dr. Sam Thomas, a fellow pastor, when he is in India and we are able to communicate, we are still unified on mission with God, even though we are not together. Pastor Julio in Haiti and I talk almost daily, at least in a texting form. When I talk to my friend in China, we still have this wonderful relationship that is strengthened under the unity of the Holy Spirit, because we have been forged at a relational level that no form of distance can fracture if our identity is found in Christ, if we are allowing our walk to be in rhythm and in concert with the Holy Spirit.

The Greek word here used for eager here is an emphatic command. It means that we are to spare no effort at being. It is a present participle, which means it is a call for continuous, diligent activity. So, when we cannot be together, that does not give us a pass on being forged. We may have to be *more* eager. We have to work *harder* to ensure that we remain connected and together.

This implies a full effort from the entire part of man. It is meant to involve His will. It is a sentiment of reason, of physical strength, and of total attitude. This does not give me a pass. This is not about being quiet or about a wait-and-see attitude. This is about deliberate, intentional initiative to be forged together.

Don't sit back and wait on others to call or to text you. Pick up the phone. *You* initiate the contact. Take the initiative. Be a catalyst, and do it today.

Those are the overtones of verse three. Those who have been given this calling, believers in Christ, are urged to race ahead, to meet a deadline, to persevere, and receive the prize. *That* is our calling.

In light of verse three, what am I so eager to accomplish? I am not talking about your eagerness to complete your spring cleaning honey-do list. I'm talking about at the core of life. What am I eager to do? Am I eager to pursue Christ? Am I eager to pursue His Word? Am I eager to lead my family? Am I eager to make a difference? Am I eager to serve my neighbors? Am I eager to carry on Gospel conversations? Am I eager to point others to Him? Am I eager to do that?

As we all strive for that, there is this forging of unity in the Spirit, and it helps us recognize when there are divisions among us. There are differences of opinions and differences in politics. There are differences in reference points and life experiences that are all part of making us unique. But, in the essentials, we must have unity, and in those other areas, we must show love.

We must walk with an unwavering commitment to work for unity and to maintain it. This drives me to care, to love, and to work through even differences. Unity in the church rises up from the unity of our God.

Forged for One

Let's read verses four, five, and six about oneness.

Ephesians 4:4-6

There is one body and one Spirit—just as you were called to the one hope that belongs to your call— one Lord, one faith, one baptism, one God and Father of all, who is over all and through all and in all.

The power of the forge is the unity and strength that comes from being exposed to the fire. We are thinking of a physical, actual forge where someone may be pounding steel. The power of that, the catalyst for that is the intensity of heat. Maybe you have never really witnessed a true forge in action, but maybe you've built a bonfire in the backyard, and it was growing strong, but it started to dwindle.

When the fire is starting to die and you want to cause it to regain its strength, what do you do? You begin to fan that flame, and you give it some wind. You may even move some of those embers to touch other logs to reignite that flame.

Why? That strength requires the fuel of wind, which in this context is the Holy Spirit, and the connection to touch others, which is this call to unity, so we can burn for Christ.

There is a connection here from what we just read to what we read earlier in verses one through three, that our calling comes through the Spirit. The church of God is an organic, living being. Believers are members, and Christ is the head, the power for us. The reason for the church's hope for and commitment to unity is deposited in Heaven. Colossians 1:3-6 says:

Colossians 1:3-6

We always thank God, the Father of our Lord Jesus Christ, when we pray for you, since we heard of your faith in Christ Jesus and of the love that you have for all the saints, because of the hope laid up for you in heaven. Of this you have heard before in the word of the truth, the gospel, which has come to you, as indeed in the whole world it is bearing fruit and increasing—as it also does among you, since the day you heard it and understood the grace of God in truth.

It is not the attainment of unity; it is the guarantee of that attainment in the best interest of the church preserved in the heavens, out of this world. No matter how separated we may be by language, race, color, station, opinion, politics, interest, circumstances or experiences, we are members of this one body in Christ. And the duty, therefore, as believers is to regard the differences not as hindrances, but as helps to the fuller development of divine truth, in the fuller manifestation of God to the church.

It is the idea of this mosaic, like those wonderful glass pictures where broken shards of glass that are different colors, shapes, and sizes assemble together. Independently, they would look like broken pieces of glass. But unified together, they make a beautiful picture.

We may appear to be just one individual, but when we step back, we see the collective whole. We are a beautiful picture representing Jesus' church, this forged body of believers. We are a picture of Christ's love to our community and to the world.

And where is the origin? It is the hope of your calling. It streams out of the call of the Spirit who urges us to a lively hope, "being himself, the seal of our inheritance (1 Peter 1:3)." We have one Father who creates one family, one Lord, Jesus, who creates one faith, one hope, and one baptism, and one spirit who is unifying us into one forged body, and the triune God, the beautiful picture of the Trinity that is over all, through all, and in all as established in verse six.

If we, together, are under the calling and lordship of Jesus, it is important to understand two aspects of what that means.

1. Ownership

One is the idea of ownership. Jesus Christ is our owner. Jesus Christ is not only the Lord of all, but He is especially the Lord of His own people. We are not our own. We have been redeemed and bought with a price, even with His precious blood. 1 Corinthians 6:20 says:

1 Corinthians 6:20

For this, and he both died, and rose, and revived, there was resurrection that he might be the Lord, both of the dead, and of the living.

2. Authority

There is also the idea of authority. There is no part of my being and no event in my life that is *not* subject to His authority. It is the subjection of all believers to one Lord that marks the unity of the church.

That is the beauty of this baptism. You identify your life with the baptism of Christ, the death, burial, and resurrection of Christ, and connect to us, as a body of believers, locally representing the hope of Christ to the world. Galatians 2:27 and 28:

Galatians 3:27-28

As many as have been baptized into Christ have put on Christ. There is neither Jew nor Greek, there is neither bond nor free, there is neither male nor female: for ye are all one in Christ Jesus.

We share this common mark that we are each sealed by the Holy Spirit, and that faith binds us and forges us at the soul level. When we are willing to look beyond the surface, beyond our interests and beyond our differences, we can clearly see what binds us.

But it requires us to not look at the external or even simply look at our character. We look deeper at the characteristics, those stones of peace, love and patience, because those are actually markers of our Creator. That is us displaying His nature and character to the world.

So, in the spirit of Ephesians 4:6, we must look ultimately to the triune God. He is our focus. He is our friend. He is our forge. Let us fix our eyes on Him and allow him to strengthen our mission, our hearts, and our hope.

Deep Dive

1. Read 2 Timothy 1:8-9. How has God called us to live, and
   what impact does that make on our testimony to others?

   _____

   _____

   _____

2. If God has called me to walk according to His will, this
   implies His authority and guidance. Read Ephesians 5:1.
   What is the benefit of His example for how we should
   live?

   _____

   _____

   _____

3. If God has called us to walk together, what are factors that
   tend to fracture our unity? What can we do about that?

   _____

   _____

   _____

Chapter Two

WORKING TOGETHER

A s we continue to look at Ephesians 4 together, my mind goes to a memory of my childhood. Maybe you can resonate with this. When I was a kid, my brother and I shared a bedroom. On the closet door was our growth chart.

We would stand up inside that closet and measure against the door. All along that door, as the years went by, there would be markers, or pins, to show how tall Alan (my brother) was on a certain date, and how tall I was. We would stand and try to get every little bit of an inch that we could.

It was a really special way to mark and measure our growth. My wife and I did the same thing with our two daughters. We had a board in a room in our house where we would measure and mark their growth with their names and dates.

It was beautiful, because it was so much more than just marks on a board. Those markers measured visible growth, but they were also benchmarks in time that measured growth in their personal lives that linked to memories in our family. It marked the maturity of us as a family unit.

I want you to take that idea, because I imagine many of you have a very similar memory. Take that idea, and just like a child's growth is measured, we are called to *grow* and mature as believers. Just like a family growth chart, whether it is on a board or a door, we mark the maturity of our family unit, so the collective growth of a church family unit displays the forged and unified presence of Christ at work.

In this chapter, we are going to continue the idea of learning the importance of God's people living and walking together in unity, on mission for God. We are going to look at verses 7 through 13 of Ephesians 4.

Fractures From Wrong Focus

Ephesians 4:7-8

But grace was given to each one of us according to the measure of Christ's gift. Therefore it says, "When he ascended on high he led a host of captives, and he gave gifts to men."

We understand the idea of giving gifts. Let's talk about what these gifts are *not*. This is not Oprah Winfrey's favorite things show where everyone gets a material gift. This is not everybody getting a stimulus check. This probably would be more comparable to Jesus' teaching of the parable of the talents, with this idea that each person has been given a resource. They are not all the same, but there is an expectation to use these gifts or talents for the advancement of the master.

Or maybe this speaks more to the idea of uniqueness. You may have read Dr. Gary Chapman's books on the power of love languages[2] and realized that we are uniquely crafted, even in the way that we give and express love. For some, giving gifts is an expression of how they give and receive love.

All of these examples draw our attention to the gift, the talent or the possession, but that is an improper focus. In fact, when we focus on the wrong things, it could lead to fractures in our unity. Our focus should not be on the gift, but instead should be on the gift *giver*.

When we read verses seven and eight of Ephesians 4, immediate attention is drawn to Christ, and according to His measure. In Ephesians 4:7, the Messiah Himself is denoted as God's gift to us. John 3:16 communicates that Jesus is a gift, and the life and the grace that He extends is a gift.

The following verses not only communicate that Jesus is a gift, but Jesus is the gift *giver*, too. We are not able to study all of Ephesians through this book; we are focusing on chapter four alone. But take time to look at chapter 1 verse 10, or chapter 2, verses 14 through 17. They point us back to the work of Christ and the gift that He has given us.

In fact, in harmony with God, Jesus distributes His gifts according to His riches. Go back to Ephesians 1:8. The Messiah's actions are characterized by generosity. He, the great gift, is demonstrated in the various gifts that the Church has received.

Back in Ephesians 3:8, it says that His gift giving is according to His unfathomable riches. And it has now been shown how He has opened the doors of His storehouses to His Church, and He distributes nothing less than grace. He is the administrator of that grace. He gives Himself freely. How amazing is that?!

But there is a warning that we have to pay attention to. We are all guilty of this around the Christmas season. The day of or a few weeks after, we're casually reconnecting with friends or family, and the question comes up: "Hey, what did you get for Christmas?"

We love to ask that question. Why? It's because our mind is so easily drawn to elevating the gift. But, the gift is not the point. Our attention must be on the giver, and in the Church, which is us, when we focus on the gift, it can cause us to be led to selfishness. It can even crack or fracture our unity, because it leads us to this attitude of comparing with one another, rather than letting our eyes and attention be fixed on God. God desires for us to be forged together in unity, and that requires a proper focus.

Let's look beyond a local expression of faith. Denominations have developed over time, and we have become divided in that one denominational group will elevate one gift set over another. But the eye doesn't make itself the eye, and the hand doesn't make itself the hand. The positions of the believers in the Church are determined not by us, but by Christ.

This grace is given, as we just read in verse seven, *according to the measure of the gift of Christ*. Christ is the source of all spiritual gifts. He determines how they are given. He determines their distribution. He determines all of it, and they are not given according to our merit or capacity. They are not given according to our desires, but according to His sovereign pleasure. *Grace* here refers to the gracious influence of the Holy Spirit given to all Christians to help them live a life of holiness.

There is therefore no room for arrogance, ego and self-inflation. There is no room for envy or jealousy because of the grace that others have received. We are given grace by Christ. The variety of gifts creates a beautiful mosaic and enhances the community. And in Ephesians 4, Paul is quoting Psalm 68.

Psalm 68 is a psalm of triumph, and it is elevating the victory of Jesus Christ, this Messiah. He finished the work of His death, burial, resurrection and His ascension that we learned of in Acts 1:9. This defining moment means all of us who were once hostages to sin now follow in this path of righteousness.

The point is simply this: Compare what we read in Psalm 68 to what we read in Ephesians 4. In any ancient wartime conquest, the victor, the conqueror, gets gifts to distribute. And so, Christ in His resurrection and ascension (you can read of that all throughout Scripture, but particularly in Ephesians 1:22), put everything under his feet and appointed Him as head over everything for the Church.

Back in the Psalm 68, specifically in verse 18, there is a reference to Christ's triumph. It notes that the victor receives homage. In Ephesians 4, it is emphasizing not the gifts that Christ is warranted to receive, but the gifts that He graciously gives. Jesus is pouring out grace on us, and we are going to see later the demonstration of that.

Focus on the gift giver, and be thankful and gracious for the grace that he has demonstrated to us. I have received what I do not deserve, which is why I love the hymn, *Grace Greater Than Our Sin*[3]:

"Marvelous grace of our loving Lord, grace that exceeds our sin, exceeds our guilt. On Calvary's Mountain, his love was outpoured there where his blood was spilled."

This grace that will pardon and cleanse within is greater than all of us, and we need to see that. Let that idea and reality marinate in your heart. It should draw us to focus on Him.

A Finished Mission

In verses 9 and 10, we see that the finished mission fills us with hope. Let's read verses 9 and 10 of Ephesians chapter four. Now, these verses have given a lot of people a lot of confusion and struggle, but we are not going to be intimidated by handling a difficult text.

Ephesians 4:9-10

In saying, "He ascended," what does it mean but that he had also descended into the lower regions, the earth? He who descended is the one who also ascended far above all the heavens, that he might fill all things.

Christ's ascension was magnified by His descension. John 3:13 reinforces the significance of this, and this is where I think this verse is problematic for some. Some may read Ephesians 4:9 and get it confused with or misinterpret it along with 1 Peter 3:19, to come to a conclusion that Jesus left the cross and went to Hell. This is a common misconception that is accepted by many. They say it means that Jesus descended to Hell following His death on the cross to preach to those there.

However, the roots of this idea actually go back to some church councils that gathered in 300 and 400 AD, well after Christ had ascended. It really found a lot of roots in Catholicism, and it resonates even today. But this is truthfully an unfounded misunderstanding of what is being taught here.

Jesus was all about his Father's business. He was all about preaching the good news, saying, "Repent for the Kingdom of Heaven is at hand," and pointing people to Himself and to the Father. Let's think about this logically. It would be contradictory and a futile exercise for Him to go to Hell to preach to a group of people whose eternal destiny was already established.

His death on the cross defeated the penalty of sin, and His resurrection would forever bring victory over death and the grave. There is way more evidence through careful and accurate exegesis of Scripture to read verses like 1Peter 3:22 and Luke 23:43, which suggest that Jesus immediately was in the presence of God upon His death.

In fact, what this verse is speaking to is ringing the bell of His incarnation, that God sent His Son Jesus from Heaven to Earth. He came to Earth, even to the lower parts, like Gethsemane, Calvary and the grave. And it was no holiday for Him to visit. It was no green pasture or no golden palace.

He was taken from prison, from judgment, and yet there He triumphed over all of His enemies. And now He is exalted far above all heavens. His descent was deep into the lower parts of

Earth, that is the grave. But His ascent was more glorious than His descent had been humbling.

The Hebrew idea of various heavens is even brought into this text in that He is far above the heavens, way above the skies and the stars. There is beauty and power in the transcendent view of the purpose of Christ; He is reigning forever.

But as majestic as His ascension was, we must be aware of the same warning that the angel delivered to the witnesses of His ascension, recorded in Acts chapter one. Do you remember when, after Jesus had ascended, the angels presented themselves to those witnesses? The angel said, "Why do you stand here gazing up into Heaven? He is coming again, and you have work to do [That's the Ricky paraphrase]."

The finished work of Christ, his descension onto Earth and into the grave, His finished mission that ascended Him into Heaven where He now sits at the right hand of the Father, having fully paid the atonement and the price of our sin that only He could do, that finished work of Christ, doesn't allow us just to stand in awe. We *should* be in awe of who He is, but just like the warning to the angels, you've got work to do. Go and share that good news with others! Multiply and be faithful to spread the hope of the Gospel to the world, because He is coming again.

Service That Multiplies

That leads us to the next point from this section of Scripture. Faithful service should multiply. You and I should recognize this gift that has come from Christ, realize its completion, and it should lead us to faithful service. In verses 11 through 13, now Paul is going to get really specific in some of these examples and encouragements to us.

Ephesians 4:11-13

And he gave the apostles, the prophets, the evangelists, the shepherds and teachers, to equip the saints for the work of ministry, for building up the body of Christ, until we all attain to the unity of the faith and of the knowledge of the Son of God, to mature manhood, to the measure of the stature of the fullness of Christ.

Let's just get really practical. Have you ever been given a gift, and that gift had a very specific purpose? When I think about this, I think about a gift card. My wife, Hilary, and I married in 1996. We were teaching school and loving life. I was coaching basketball at the time in Columbus, GA.

I think the only upscale restaurant in town was on Veteran's Parkway, and I think it was a bar and grill called The Garlic Clove. We were given a gift card by the parents of the basketball team that year to The Garlic Clove.

I remember opening the envelope, and it was for $80. I'm going to be honest with you; my idea of a nice restaurant growing up was either Tuesdays at Del Taco, or if we were really getting fancy, Applebee's. That was my idea of a nice restaurant.

And so, I remember opening up that gift card for $80. I looked to Hilary and said, "How many times can we eat on this? There's no way a meal can be $80!" I thought that until we walked into

The Garlic Clove in 1996 and realized that on the menu were things like escargot and steak. Needless to say, we had to put a little bit of our own money in with this $80, but it was a memorable meal.

I tell you that story to acknowledge the idea that we sometimes are given a gift out of love, but that gift is intended for a very specific thing. It can only be used in this one place for this one thing.

As we look in verses 11 through 13, we are going to see a demonstration of specific gifts that are given for very specific purposes. And the idea is that they grow and multiply the Kingdom of God, because that is why we are commissioned to be on mission. The ultimate end of these gifts are to run the race that has been set out for us, individually and collectively. It reminds me of the words of Hebrews 12:1-3.

Hebrews 12:1-3

Therefore, since we also have such a large cloud of witnesses surrounding us, let us lay aside every weight and the sin that so easily ensnares us. Let us run with endurance the race that lies before us, keeping our eyes on Jesus, the source and perfecter of our faith, who for the joy that lay before Him endured a cross and despised the shame and has sat down at the right hand of God's throne.

The power of that verse as it relates to what we're talking about is, our focus must be fixed on Him so that we don't become fractured in recognizing our own desires. Instead, we focus on *His* desires, and as we individually and collectively follow the path that He has charted for us, we advance His mission. It causes us to be faithful to that service and to multiply. Then in verses 11 and 12, it goes back in time to lead us forward. It even lays out some examples of the Apostles of old, who laid the foundation of our faith as they wrote the New Testament.

The prophets of the Old Testament cried out for repentance, and they all pointed to God. The evangelists of old, and even of the new world, blazed the trail to take the Gospel to places and to people who had never heard it before. And then it refers to the pastors, the shepherds and teachers who operate not in an evangelistic mode, but in a stationary mode to care for and disciple those under their care to pursue Christ.

And all of these that are described are designed to build God's church and to strengthen the body of Christ, or equip the saints to be mobilized on mission with God. It uses the language of ministry here. In fact, this challenge is not just to a select few, but it is to all believers. The equipping implies a continuous, ongoing work to continue until the Lord's return.

Well, what does this mean? When we look at this word in the original language, in its original context, katartismos (it only occurs here in the New Testament, by the way), derives from a verb that means to reconcile, bring together, or even in surgery, to set bones straight. More generally, it means to restore, prepare or create. And so, here we realize that we are challenged, mobilized, and on mission to equip one another to set things straight, to reconcile, to restore, to prepare and to create.

Ephesians 4:12 itself provides a clarification. In other terms, by the men appointed by Christ (verse 11), the saints are being prepared for a specific task. But then, it begs the question, what could that task or that ministry be? The word ministry is taken in this large sense to signify general spiritual service.

Spiritual Exercises

This is not specifically talking about the list of spiritual gifts. This is a little more broad, beyond just the spiritual gifts. This is not intended to be exhaustive, but let me offer some ministry areas that you may consider some unique spiritual exercises that Scripture defines for us.

1. Service (Hebrews 6:10)
2. Prayer and Preaching (Acts 6:4)
3. Relief to Your Community (Acts 11:29)
4. Serving the Church Family (1 Corinthians 16:15)
5. Generosity (2 Corinthians 9:12-13)
6. Financial Support for Full-time Ministers
(2 Corinthians 11:8)
7. Support of Others (2 Timothy 4:11)

Every believer is equipped and challenged to be fruitful in every good work. All of the works are important. And this is where that warning way back at the very beginning comes in and where the potential fracture can come in. We sometimes elevate one exercise over another or allow some comparison or greed to come in.

All are important. No matter your giftedness, you and I are en-couraged, challenged and commanded to serve, which is why we, at my church, say, "Every member is a minister, and every

WORKING TOGETHER · 37

member should have a ministry." I encourage you to consider where and how you should be serving the people of God.

Be wary of prioritizing one over the other and elevating people who may be more public in their service. They are all important. The beauty of it is that it results in a church that glorifies God above all and grows in Spirit.

It is this idea of regeneration. It's like if you plant a garden and specifically use an heirloom seed. That seed, when it develops into a plant, can be regenerated to grow more plants.

The church is an organism. It is a living body of faith that loves, serves and cares. It is designed to reproduce and multiply. But in order for the church to multiply, it requires the individual believer to grow. We see in verse 13 this idea of maturity. For the sake of the whole body of believers, I should, as an individual, strive to grow, to become a healthy part of this body of believers and to demonstrate maturity for the body's sake, not just for my own. And you should strive for the same thing.

So, this is us being forged together, stronger and stronger, both for the individual and for the whole. It is the stature of the fullness of Christ. Compare that to Romans 8:29, which says, "Whom He did foreknow, them He also ordained to be conformed to the image of His Son." The more I grow, the more I mature and look like Him. And the more we as a collective body are forged into that idea of serving, growing, pursuing, and practicing, we all look more like Him.

Measuring Maturity

Let's go back to where we started and the idea of a childhood growth chart. Here are three quick ways we measure maturity in the Church.

1. Unity of faith

The first sign would be unity of faith. This expression continues from verses three through six, and we are carrying that idea here with specific emphasis on the unified belief in the knowledge of the Son of God.

Have you ever spent time with a group of people who all cheered for the same sports team? Now, I realize this is a really shallow example, but I think you'll get it. There is evident unity when you are around other people who share a common interest or a common belief. There is unity that comes from a common expression of faith.

2. Knowledge of Christ

Second is the knowledge of the Son of God, or specifically the knowledge of Christ. Let's compare this to Colossians 2:2-3, where it says:

Colossians 2:2-3

That their hearts may be encouraged, being knit together in love, to reach all the riches of full assurance of under-standing and of the knowledge of God's mystery, which is Christ in whom are hidden all the treasures of wisdom and of knowledge."

Here's the idea: Your personal and disciplined pursuit of Christ develops your faith, and it develops the faith of those around you. Dads, when you chase hard after Jesus and then begin to pastor your family more effectively, they will begin to pursue hard after Jesus. It is a demonstration of multiplication and of regeneration.

3. Evidence of Growth in Christ

Third, there is evidence of growth in Christ. The goal here is for the Church to be its very best, to be complete. And these verses in Ephesians 4:7-13 really compare well to Colossians 1:28 where it says, "So that we may present every person complete in Christ."

All of us want to grow. We are diligently working to prepare ourselves for Christ's return. If you are in doubt of how soon that could be, just look around you; just pay attention to the news. There are more reminders today than I have ever seen in my lifetime that the return of Christ is imminent, and I am so excited. But, it is a reminder of the need for us to work diligently. We've got work to do.

Ultimately, the fullness of maturity cannot even be expressed in this lifetime; it can only be fully perfected in Glory. The Bible nowhere shows the perfection of the Church occurring on this Earth. The Church is to be without spot, wrinkle or blemish when the day of His glorious presentation comes.

The design of the Church and the Christian ministry is to labor, mature and grow... but perfection will come later. That is why we sing about eternity with Him. It brings into perspective the reality and the reminder penned in 1 Corinthians 13. "Now we see but a poor reflection, but then we will see clearly."

I long for the day when I can worship Him face to face. But until that day comes, I love the opportunity to be strengthened by the unity of other believers. You make me more like Jesus, and I hope to help you look more like Him, too, so that we together can be a picture of unity to a world that is broken and fractured and so that we can be ready for the groom when He comes for His bride.

Here is the question: If you were to step up to a spiritual growth chart, would the marker at the top of your head really signify any measurable growth? When you and I flex those spiritual muscles, exercise those gifts, serve others, put others above ourselves, work to be more like Him and realize that God gives grace, we can grow.

Your growth doesn't just benefit you. Your spiritual health can benefit the body when we walk in unity and we together pursue serving Him, forged together.

Deep Dive

1. Read Ephesians 4:7-8. If Christ is the gift-giver, why are we jealous of others' gifts rather than trusting Christ's plan?

    _____

    _____

    _____

2. Read John 3:13-15. Why is it crucial that our focus is on Jesus and that we point others to Him?

    _____

    _____

    _____

3. Ephesians 4:11-13 paints a picture of a growing church that is exercising its gifts. How has God gifted you to serve His Church and how can you maximize that gift for His glory?

    _____

    _____

Chapter Three

GROWING TOGETHER

I grew up playing a lot of basketball. There were many, many days I spent on my house basketball court (really just a dirt side yard with a basketball goal on it), trying to develop my skills. My eighth grade year, I decided to go out for our JV basketball team, and I barely made it. I was one of two alternatives who made the team, and I was so excited.

I was happy that I made it, but here was the reality: At that time, I was a skinny, six-foot-one kid. I hadn't really grown all the way yet, and I was a typical lanky, uncoordinated eighth grader.

My mind and my heart commitment were there, but my physical ability had not yet grown into my size 13 shoes. I made the team, but needless to say, I was an uncoordinated middle-schooler, and I often heard these dreaded words: "He has great potential."

Now, let me just tell you; we may offer that to a student or a kid as a word of encouragement, but truthfully, for a guy like me, it's humiliating. Basically, it is just a polite way of saying, "Good try, Son. You're not quite there." ---But I had great *potential*.

So far, we have learned that the body of Christ should work and strive for unity and maturity. In this chapter, we're going to continue that idea with a picture of what *immaturity* looks like and go more in depth into how Christ calls us to grow.

In Ephesians 4, I really want to slow down and drill into three verses that help us understand the importance of maturity and its impact on our ability to be forged together, because here is the truth: Your individual growth and maturity directly impact the maturity of the whole faith family.

Delayed Growth

First, let's talk about the idea of delayed growth. We see this in verse 14:

Ephesians 4:14

...so that we may no longer be children, tossed to and fro by the waves and carried about by every wind of doctrine, by human cunning, by craftiness in deceitful schemes.

There is hard scientific data that suggests a person's move from childhood into adolescence is getting earlier and earlier. Sometimes by the age of 10, a kid begins entering into the stage of adolescent growth. Depending on your gender, this season of growth can go all the way up to about age 24.

While physical and emotional development vary from person to person, there comes a time when mentally, someone has to make the decision to put away childish behavior and grow up.

Listen, I enjoy and find pleasure in watching a kid be a kid. In fact, I think sometimes as a culture, we may not allow kids to be kids long enough. That's another social conversation for another day. But here's what is frustrating: when a grown adult acts like a child.

This may be an adult man who whines when he doesn't get his way. This could be two adults who argue and bicker with one another like two middle-schoolers. Childish individualism drives people apart and truthfully, it shatters unity.

Ephesians 4 points to this idea of delayed spiritual growth and its impact on an individual, as well as a need to understand that it has an impact on the body, the fellowship of the Church. Some of the original readers of this letter that Paul wrote to the church in Ephesus who were born again, had put their trust and faith in Jesus and had been regenerated at the soul level, had not yet grown up into spiritual adulthood.

The challenge here in verse 14 is that we see the results, or the dangerous implications, of delayed spiritual growth. Here are some examples:

Unanchored

The verse specifically uses the language of "tossed to and fro". It gives us imagery of being tossed about in a storm. It makes me think of a boat that is unanchored. When I was studying this passage, I thought about how my family loves to take a boat out to Lake Harding at the dam and watch the fireworks on July 4th.

There are so many boats in the water for that event that when you get out there and are enjoying the moment, if your boat is not anchored, you will find yourself moving, shifting or coming close to hitting other boats.

The point is, if we are not intentional about being anchored, we can be tossed into a place where we can unintentionally hit other people. If you are unanchored, you may drift into areas you don't want to be in. An unanchored life is a life that is tossed and threatened by crisis, stress or trends in culture. We may be easily swayed from one opinion to the next. However, unintended outcomes can be avoided when we are committed to exercise discernment and build discipline into our life.

Drifting

If we have delayed growth, we can also drift. That is the idea describing the result of someone who is not drilled down into something that can hold them steady. A person who doesn't drill down can be carried away into confusion and disunity.

Let me give you some examples of what may impact or be a catalyst to this drifting. Here in Ephesians 4:14, we see "carried away by every wind of doctrine," and the singular word used for *doctrine* here in verse 14 suggests a level of Christian teaching that should not be taken to suggest that the winds of false teaching are blowing from outside the church. The New Testament shows that believers were under continual pressure from *inside* the church.

1. Fierce Wolves

Fierce wolves could come and impact what was being taught. In fact, so you know I'm not just making this up, look at Acts 20:29-30 (Paul writing):

Acts 20:29-30

I know that after my departure fierce wolves will come in among you, not sparing the flock; and from among your own selves will arise men speaking twisted things, to draw away the disciples after them.

This is a warning that from inside the church, you and I need to filter what we hear and say with what the Word of God says. This is the filter through which we can find an anchor in Christ. 1 Thessalonians 5:21 tells us, "Test everything. Hold fast what is good."

What does that mean, practically? With anybody who is teaching (it could be a life group leader or me teaching and preaching on a Sunday morning), filter what you hear through what the Word of God says. Test everything, and hold on to what is good.

Do not just follow what someone says. It's what the Word of God says that allows us to be anchored and not tossed to and fro. The filter of Scripture can help us avoid drifting, and it can also help us identify false teachers.

2. False Teachers

False teachers were marked by selfishness and deceit. Many times in the New Testament this can be found, such as in Romans 16, Colossians 2, Galatians 2 and 2 Corinthians 2. The word translated here as *trickery* is literally derived from the idea of playing a game with a loaded set of dice.

Basically, playing dice with a loaded hand where you know you are going to get the outcome you want out of selfishness and deceit. It is the exact imagery used here of cunning, craftiness and deceitful schemes. If we are not careful, it can be seen by false teachers and communicators who are actually communicating a false gospel.

For example, false gospels are ones that imply that salvation is not by faith alone (Ephesians 2:8-9). Please understand; Jesus is all you need. Jesus plus anything is a dangerous path to walk down. Loaded dice may be hints of a prosperity gospel that leads you to the idea that if you just name and claim a blessing from God or you follow God with enough enthusiasm and diligence, He is going to bless you financially. That is not biblical.

Anything that adds to the purity of the Gospel message from one God, one Lord, one faith and one baptism is wrong. We need to understand that there is a warning here. There is a potential threat to our unity if we are not anchored solidly in the Gospel and in the truth of Scripture. We may be tempted to follow a fierce wolf that teaches a false truth.

I believe everybody wants to be mature; everybody wants to grow. This is part of our human nature. In fact, you may have a picture of yourself as a child or have seen your kids walking around in their parents' boots.

My experience has been that when small children spend time with adults, they tend to act like that older person. It is wired in us to be drawn out into our growth. In fact, when we observe someone who is older acting younger, it is a red flag and a turnoff.

Every believer I've ever met who truly has put his or her trust in Jesus desires to grow; they want to mature. But the question is one of discipline, of full submission to Christ or of not really knowing *how* to grow.

We have just looked here at this idea of delayed growth in verse 14, where Paul paints a negative picture. Now let's turn to verse 15, where he is going to give us a positive comparison. A key word here is the first word of verse 15 of *rather*. He is playing a contrast game, moving from delayed growth in verse 14 to coordinated growth.

Coordinated Growth

Ephesians 4:15

Rather, speaking the truth in love, we are to grow up in every way into him who is the head, into Christ.

Let's go back to where I started with my personal story of being a kid playing on my dirt basketball court. I loved basketball, and therefore, I was a huge Michael Jordan fan. A lot of people have watched the ESPN documentary called *The Last Dance*[4]. In that film, one thing you learn is that Michael Jordan, arguably the greatest basketball player of all time, was cut his sophomore year in high school. He didn't even make the team!

His response to that was, between his sophomore and junior year, he worked really hard because his mom pushed him to do so. And he grew four inches that one year. He came back his junior year, four inches taller, and his uncoordinated self had grown into his body a little bit more. He was a different player. He had hit a growth spurt, and it made a huge impact.

Here is the idea and why I even draw that comparison: When we hit a spiritual growth spurt, it is awesome to see, and other people can tell. They can notice the difference. Believers ought to be well grounded in the truth, not like a baby or an infant or a delayed adolescent, but reflecting our full age.

Proclaim Truth

But how does this happen? How do we have this coordinated individual growth, and what impact does it have on being forged as a body of believers? The first idea we see from verse 15 is a bold proclamation of the truth.

Truth is the element by which we are to live, to move and to have our being (Acts 17:28). Jesus even identifies Himself in John 14:6 by saying, "I am the way, the truth and the life." Faithfulness to the truth is the backbone of Christian ministry. But truth is inseparably married to love.

Good tidings spoken harshly are not good tidings. The truth refers primarily to the Gospel, to Christian doctrine, to the Word of God itself. The truth is then the standard by which we judge all other teachings. It is an understanding and knowledge of proclaiming the truth that helps us identify what is false. We need to value and understand the truth. Therefore, we need to value and understand the Gospel and the teachings of Christ. Knowing the truth will help you have an anchor that you can cling to and avoid being tossed to and fro.

"Speaking the truth in love" that we see here in Ephesians 4:15 is literally translated "truthing in love". It includes the notion of maintaining the truth in love, living the truth in love and doing the truth in love.

Another way you could say it is, know the truth, live the truth, speak the truth. But what we need to understand is that there is a connection between our beliefs and our actions. It causes me to then ask this honest question of myself, and I encourage you to internalize this question as well: What does your life, your actions and your testimony say of your love for Jesus Christ?

The speaker is to the truth as an easel is to the painting or as a candlestick is to the light. In other words, our life, our actions and our testimony give credibility to our message. Or on the flip side, our life and our actions can hinder our message. The truth entrusted to the Church is the truth of an all-conquering love. And where there is no love, the truth revealed by God is often rejected.

Thank God that there are some churches who are determined at all costs to defend and uphold God's revealed truth. That's great. But sometimes they are conspicuously lacking in love. It is almost like the Incredible Hulk imagery. When they smell or sniff anything that smells of heresy, their noses begin to twitch; their muscles begin to rip up, and they are ready to come out and war over it. They seem to enjoy nothing more than to fight.

On the opposite side, there are others who make another mistake. They are determined at all costs to maintain and express brotherly love. But in order to do that, they are prepared even to sacrifice the very central truths and the core of who God is and what He has revealed to us. What I want us to see is, both of those extremes are unbalanced and unbiblical. Truth becomes hard if it is not softened by love, and love becomes soft if it is not strengthened by truth. We have to speak the truth in love.

Core Training

Coordinated growth also comes through core training. Verse 15 implies that growth leads to a closer relationship to Christ, and unity flows from that. The two react to one another.

If you work out or have followed any strength and physical fitness training, you have learned a lot about the importance of a strong core for posture and stability. Similarly, we are challenged to grow up in every way with special attention to the core of our faith.

Perhaps today when you evaluate yourself and look internally, you say, "I feel pretty strong and mature as a Christian. I feel pretty solid in my faith." If so, that's great. But, we all have cracks. We all have weak areas. We all have a need for growth. I would say to help determine where those are, identify the inconsistencies in your life between your spiritual thought and your moral conduct. Those inconsistencies may reveal markers where you need to grow.

The apostle Paul, arguably next to Christ the most influential person in the New Testament, even said of himself in Romans 7, "I've got a lot of areas in my life where I need to grow." Here are some core areas of growth that we all may need to work on to mature.

1. Increase in Knowledge

An increase of knowledge, learning, or understanding is the first. We need the ability to connect the dots between one truth in Scripture to another as we study the Word. Let me illustrate it this way: I love to step out into my backyard and look up into the night sky. I'm amazed by the stars; they are beautiful. A year or two ago, my family went on a vacation to Los Angeles, and there we took advantage of the opportunity at night to go up to the Griffith Observatory on the top of a small mountain (a big hill) right in the heart of LA.

There is this beautiful observatory where you can walk and put your eye on a massive telescope. Let me just tell you about the increase of knowledge! When I look at the sky through the lens of a telescope, it is much more vast than what I am able to experience and see with my naked eye.

Just looking into the night sky with my own eye, I may stand in awe and see tens or thousands of stars. But if I look with an increase of knowledge, through a focused and intense lens of a telescope, I see that there is incredible depth to the sky.

Our understanding is like that. At first, I may see as a young Christian. As a growing Christian, I may have limited understanding of how to handle the Scriptures, and I can articulate the truth. But the more I increase in my knowledge and understanding of studying Scripture, it allows me to see much more detail and clearly into the depths of what Scripture is teaching. This comes through individual, determined, disciplined reading and studying of Scripture.

That leads me to increased knowledge into God and His plan. This is not like some magic pill. It takes some work to grow and to study God's Word.

2. Stability of Belief

The second core area of growth is a stability of our belief. Notice how these are linked together. When I deliberately exercise the discipline of studying God's Word and increase in knowledge of who He is, it develops a stable belief because I am anchoring more and more to truth. Do you see the connection? I then begin to move beyond doubt to security. I move from insecurity to security. The more I understand Him, the better I understand me.

3. Truthful

This leads to the third area of core training: truth. I am not going to spend a lot of time on this point because we talked about it just a few paragraphs ago, of speaking the truth and being honest with one another.

4. Love

Love is a character trait of God that we share, having been made in His image. 1 John 4 speaks so much about how love is from God, and everyone who loves the Word of God, knows God. There is a huge connection to me of learning to love more and love deeply and love intently as I mature and grow. That means loving myself, loving others, loving my neighbor and even, yes, loving my enemy.

Vertical Trust

In addition to core training, we must train in vertical trust. This vertical relationship we have is linked to Jesus Christ in verse 15 as the perfect example that we are to follow. He is the head. He is in charge, growing up bodily in Him, the body derives vital substance from Him. He is our source of truth. He is our source of hope. He is our source of strength.

I realize that as a pastor, I may be an instrument to challenge and teach you to grow. But Jesus Himself is the greatest source of growth in truth. The growth to be promoted is growth that is unto Him and in Him. He is the head. All of our vital substance, all of our spiritual influence, should be in Christ.

Think of it as the brain in a body and how every nerve in our physical body is connected back to that source. In fact, I would say that elevating Jesus is the starting point for a biblical unity. That is the whole purpose of Ephesians 4. This is the whole intent of this *Forged* book. It is to see the importance of us being forged and strengthened together in unity. It comes when we have our eyes fixed on Jesus as the author and the perfecter of our faith (Hebrews 12:1-2).

Elevating Jesus is the starting point for biblical unity.

What I want us to see here as we move on into verse 16 is that our vertical trust, our vertical relationship with Jesus links us to a healthy, horizontal relationship with other believers. What we will see then in verse 16 is this idea of exponential growth.

Exponential Growth

Look again at the progression. In verse 14, we push against *delayed growth*. We commit to exercise discipline so that we personally, individually experience *coordinated growth*. Then, we as a collective faith family can witness and experience *exponential growth*. We see it in the first few words of verse 16.

Ephesians 4:16

...from whom the whole body, joined and held together by every joint with which it is equipped, when each part is working properly, makes the body grow so that it builds itself up in love.

A healthy, horizontal relationship with other believers thrives and follows a healthy vertical relationship with Jesus Christ. All that the body of Christ is, has and does is determined by its both passive and active relationship with the head, that is Christ. As one man grows in faith, the army of God grows with it. When I was studying through this, I was reminded of one of my favorite books.

John Maxwell wrote a book that has been around for a while called *The 21 Irrefutable Laws of Leadership*[5]. If you have never read it, I encourage you to do so. Or if it has been a while, shake the dust off and read it again. It is really applicable. But he has a chapter in there on raising the lid of leadership, this challenge that we push ourselves to grow more.

Maxwell is talking about it in the context of leadership, but I think in today's understanding, as we study Ephesians 4, verses 14, 15, and 16, that same illustration is there. I can never be satisfied or content with my level of spiritual maturity; I must constantly be pushing myself to grow more, to increase in knowledge, understanding and stability in the truth and increase in love, because as I grow, those around me grow with me.

Dads, as you grow in your pursuit of Christ, your family grows. Leaders in your organization, entrepreneurs, managers at work, as you grow, those around you grow. Life group leaders, as you pursue and understand Scripture more and teach it well, your group begins to grow.

It is infectious, contagious and a natural byproduct. The challenge of horizontal growth occurs when we look to one another and spur one another on.

This is because we are united in purpose. We see this in verse 16; we are joined and held together. This is not a mere individual action. We are an organism. We are a living part of a larger body being adapted and joined to one another and held together. I am not going to spend the time to get too technical in the original language. I just want you to understand that the participle of this word is intended for this to be a process that is *continuous*. It is ongoing, never complete.

In the church, we need to understand there is tremendous diversity in spiritual growth, and we celebrate that. There are babies in Christ. There are spiritual young men and women who have been following Jesus for just a couple of years. There are also some who have grown in intellect, discipline and in faith that have been following Jesus for decades.

It is this symbiotic relationship, as we work together, jointly fitting together in this continual process to grow and please Him as we mature and learn to work with and for one another with no one despising the giftedness of someone else. Each member is in relation with the others, as well as with the head, that is Christ. Each is dependent on each other.

We are united in one purpose, as we are equipped for a mission. We all have been gifted as God designed us for the purpose of building up and edifying the body. But every part of the body has some gift, all for the same end: to glorify God and grow His kingdom on Earth as it is in Heaven. All of us ought to live in harmony together, keeping this view and grand mission in mind.

Recently, my two daughters and I went to watch the Columbus Youth Orchestra, and I'll be honest; what I expected was not what I experienced. I went expecting a bunch of middle school and high school kids to be playing string and brass instruments poorly. I expected it to be atrocious. But I experienced a beautiful harmony of these skilled musicians making this beautiful sound in concert. They had worked hard to work properly together.

The idea of verse 16 is to be working together, to be at work, to provide sustenance and to enable one another. In a healthy church, there is a continual, ongoing work of building up and constructing, not destructing. It is our work to promote peace, purity, prayerfulness, trust, truth and activity in the work of the Lord. And this is all done in love. In the absence of growth, there is decline instead of progress, death instead of life.

The question is, then, how is this growth measured? Remember Chapter 2. We are building on what we talked about when we literally used this growth chart that you may have had as a child. Measurement is important.

But, verse 16 challenges us to consider quality over quantity. The quality is measured in what is done in love. John Calvin said it this way: "Without the rule of love, the church is not built, but is dispersed."

Christ is the subject of this long sentence over these three verses that makes the church grow. He is our source of truth. He is our reason to love. He is our head and our anchor. We are continuously forged together in love as we pursue Christ.

You cannot strengthen your horizontal relationships without prioritizing your vertical relationship with Jesus. This goes to church health. This goes to the life group health. This goes to your marriage. This goes to your work relationships. Ephesians 4:14 and 3:16 are clear in their emphasis on Christ and His impact on a forged church that proclaims the truth in love.

Deep Dive

1. Ephesians 4:14 describes a believer who is slow to grow and is tempted to be drawn off course. What are some ways that a believer could be tempted in his or her beliefs and practice of faith?

_____

_____

_____

2. Ephesians 4:15 paints a picture of a growing believer who holds tight to truth. How would you define the Gospel? Read Isaiah 53:4-6, Romans 3:23-24, 1 Corinthians 15:3-4, Philippians 2:4-8, and Titus 3:4-7 to help.

_____

_____

_____

3. Ephesians 4:16 helps us see the beauty of the Church growing together. What can you do today to encourage other believers to grow and serve in love?

_____

_____

_____

Chapter Four

STRONGER TOGETHER

I n this chapter, we are going to explore the challenge of what it means to put *off* something and put *on* something else. We are going to see a sense of determination and emphasis that Paul communicates when trying to grab the attention of the reader.

We live in tension every day between how God has called us to live and what our nature pulls us toward. I'll confess to you; I struggle with this. I struggle with it every day. For me, it manifests itself in pride, stress, insecurity, ego, and even at times in a level of anger. Perhaps for you, it manifests itself in anxiety, addiction, or even in gluttony.

This struggle is not new. In fact, Paul, the same man who wrote the book of Ephesians, also described this tension in Romans 7, this internal frustration of doing the things he knows he shouldn't do, and then not being able to do the things he desires to do, or that he felt God would desire him to do. Does that sound familiar?

Be encouraged, because we can be victorious. And as believers, we are forged together, even through this struggle. We all struggle with this, and while it may manifest or look different in each one of us, we are forged together by sharing in this common struggle between the life that we are to push away from and the life that we are to draw into. "Put on and put off" is the language that we see here in Ephesians 4. I hope that we can find challenge, encouragement, and unity through this common struggle.

March To the Beat of a Different Drum

In this section of Ephesians 4, we first see that we need to march to the beat of a different drum. Let's read verses 17 through 19:

Ephesians 4:17-19

Now this I say and testify in the Lord, that you must no longer walk as the Gentiles do, in the futility of their minds. They are darkened in their understanding, alienated from the life of God because of the ignorance that is in them, due to their hardness of heart. They have become callous and have given themselves up to sensuality, greedy to practice every kind of impurity.

Paul is building on this challenge from the previous verses. We are no longer to live as children. In the last chapter, we talked about the idea of delayed adolescence. He continues in that line of thinking with this really strong emphasis. He begins in verse 17 with, "Now this I say," which is another way of saying, "I insist that you pay attention. This is so important. I can't let you miss this."

He insists that the Christian audience (he is speaking to believers) conduct themselves in a way that pleases God, and not like (he says here) the Gentiles or the pagans. In other words, that group of people who do not have a mind of God, nor for God.

I realize that for us, *pagan* and *Gentile* are not in our everyday language. But keep in mind that the challenge here is one of maturity, growing into spiritual adulthood. So Paul is, in essence, insisting and testifying in the Lord that you live differently. First, he indicates what we are *not* to be. "Don't be conformed to this world."

There is a rhythm or a cadence to the world that we are warned to avoid. Maybe you struggle with clapping and keeping rhythm. That is not the kind of rhythm or pattern that we are talking about here. Every one of us marches or lives our life in a certain pattern, cadence or rhythm.

The Rhythm of the World Leads to:

What we need to understand is, there is a significant difference or contrast to the rhythm of the Spirit in our life, as opposed to the rhythm of selfishness or the rhythm of the world. Paul is first focusing on what we should avoid, helping us see that the rhythm of the world leads to a certain mindset.

1. Emptiness

There are four things he points out here. The first one is futility. I would use the language of emptiness. It describes an empty aim or an empty pursuit in life. This is not implying simply wasting time, because we all do that from time to time, and sometimes we need to just unwind. That is not the level of emptiness here. This is not even the level of emptiness like every man has when we sit in a space and think about absolutely nothing. That's not what this is talking about.

This is the mindset of a person's heart that has reached the place where he or she can't find any purpose. This is the idea of emptiness in a void direction in life. He describes that here as futility.

2. Darkness

Paul goes on and uses the language of darkness, "darkened in their understanding." This is literally as if you had to live in a completely blacked out room, blind to everything, no light. This is the idea of being ignorant of God, ignorant in the way of salvation or ignorant in the love of Christ. This is the mindset of a person's heart who is so confused in his or her mental or emotional black hole that he or she cannot find a way out. This person may have heard of light, but can't seem to find it.

3. Excluded

Notice the demise, the weight of the description here. Emptiness, darkness, and then he even uses a word of being alienated, which I translated to the idea of feeling excluded due to a hardened heart. It may be through worldly living or selfish ambition, but this person's heart has become so insensitive to spiritual influences, he or she even perceives that there is no beauty in the divine.

This mindset in a person's heart has so closed off hope in faith that he or she has become hardened to the point of not considering faith to be an option. This person has become so hard that he or she can't listen to the truth. This is the person who, as you try to talk about God, immediately puts up a wall and says, "I don't want to hear about that anymore."

I remember trying to have a Gospel conversation with a gentleman, and it seemed like with any offer of hope or any wisdom from Scripture I tried to impart, he just pushed back and completely blocked it off, because for him, he had been very wounded. He grew up Catholic, and he was so wounded by an experience as a child in the Catholic Church that it had led him to a place of alienating any truth. He was not willing to perceive, hear or even attempt to understand. His conscience had been as if it were seared with a hot iron.

This person is someone who has been mentally or emotionally so scarred by experience or perception, he or she can't see reality anymore. Excluded. But notice how these continue to build on one another.

4. Callous

Finally, in verse 19 it leads to a point of being callous, callous to sin. Rough, calloused hands show someone who is willing to work, and that's admirable. But here, the word suggests it is at the soul level, and the person ceases to even feel.

Maybe this person developed in a cold or a confused value system that led them to a point of reckless abandonment in conduct or hedonism in the way he or she deals with sensuality or influence.

Interestingly, Paul is writing to a group of people who lived in the city of Ephesus, and Ephesus was known for its idol worship. It was known for its cultic religion. It was known because the temple of Artemis there was one of impurity, fornication and self-expression; It was just rampant.

What I want us to understand is, as Paul describes this mindset of callousness and being in denial and darkness, this is not exclusive to the culture of the Ephesians. In fact, we need to recognize this was not a unique problem to the Christians in that culture.

It is strikingly similar to our world today. We live in a place where postmodern philosophies, values and opinions have blurred our understanding of right and wrong. We are full of narcissism, which is being so self-absorbed in what *I* feel and look like, that pleasure takes priority over everything.

Even now we are beginning to see language of deconstructed faith, which breaks down any anchoring belief in a form of nihilism that holds to life having no value or purpose.

I realize I just threw a lot of big words out there, but you don't have to look around very far to see where the pattern of the world in which we live is strikingly similar to the pattern of the world that is described in Ephesians 4. And here we stand, much like those Christians Paul was writing this letter to, today with a warning of how we should avoid living, and then a reminder that the world we live in does not define the way we live.

The world in which you live does not have to define how *you* live. It certainly can, but rather than the pattern of the world or the rhythm of the world defining how we live, Jesus should.

Culture changes, but Jesus doesn't. We even change, but Jesus doesn't. And we need to march to the rhythm and the pattern of the Holy Spirit and choose to anchor our thoughts, dreams and values on Him rather than on culture or trends.

Make a Big Deal Out of Jesus

What this challenges us to do, then, is to make a really big deal out of Jesus. Let's read verses 20 and 21.

Ephesians 4:20-21

But that is not the way you learned Christ!—assuming that you have heard about him and were taught in him, as the truth is in Jesus.

What is something that is a really big deal in our world today? My mind immediately goes to high school graduation. This is one of those rites of passage that we experience every year. I am so sad for the seniors of the class of 2020, "the COVID class," as they will always be known. There were so many of these experiences that were well-deserved that they did not get to experience.

Here's the point: As much as seniors are excited about graduation from high school, for them it is so much more about not having to walk back through the doors of high school in August. It is a really big deal. This is a cultural rite of passage into adulthood. This is a generational gift that many take for granted.

In fact, if you probe around in your immediate or extended family, you likely have someone in your family, maybe a parent or a grandparent, who was the first ever in your family to graduate from high school. And because that has moved from being the exception to now the rule, I think we have lost sight of how much of a big deal it really is to graduate high school.

So what does this have to do with anything in Ephesians 4, you might ask? Well, a lot really. You see, sometimes we see and hear of something so much that we come to accept it as commonplace. We may lose the significance of the moment. We may lose sight of how big of a deal it is.

Perhaps we see and hear of Jesus so often that we lose sight of just how big of a deal He really is. Perhaps we have become so accustomed to saying His name, or maybe even taking His name in vain, we lose sight of how big of a deal He really is.

Here in verse 20, the expression Paul uses is, "We have learned Christ." That is a full and packed thought, because life is really all about Christ. It is all about His influence, and that is so woven through songs we sing of the supremacy of Christ, the sovereignty of Christ, the lordship of Christ and his kingship.

Learning Christ is so much more than just learning doctrine, memorizing a ritual, quoting a command or reciting a verse from the Bible. It has much more to do with knowing Christ personally, not simply knowing *about* Him. It is the difference between reading a book and actually having been there.

It is not enough to know *about* Christ. The challenge here is to know Him more personally and more intimately in this relational pursuit of Him. And He is the trustworthy guide for ordering a Christian way of life.

In contrast, we see here that when we learn Christ, we realize that truth apart from Christ is unstable. It is unstable when I try to find truth in anything other than Him, because as He says of Himself in John 14:6, "I am the way, the truth, and the life. No one comes to the Father, but by me."

Truth apart from Christ is unstable, and the foundation of your life matters. The foundation of the Church matters. Some of you may have been on the beach recently. While I love that sensation of standing on the edge of the ocean and allowing sand to be pulled out from underneath my feet because that is a soothing, satisfying feeling, that is not a good foundation on which to build anything.

Measure Growth By Markers Of Change

Rather than the sinking sand, I need to build my life on the solid rock of Jesus. I love the truth of the hymn that says, "My hope is built on nothing less than Jesus' blood righteousness." That anchor will allow me to truly measure growth in my life by defined markers of change.

We have all throughout Ephesians 4 used this measured growth. And we are going to define what some of those look like when we read verses 22 through 24.

Ephesians 4:22

...to put off your old self, which belongs to your former manner of life and is corrupt through deceitful desires, and to be renewed in the spirit of your minds, and to put on the new self, created after the likeness of God in true righteousness and holiness.

Have you ever done any spring cleaning? Spring is the time of year when we normally do major cleaning, or you are swapping out your closet for your spring clothes. Many of us are set on making change or bringing fresh life. The grass and flowers sprout in spring, and what has gone from brown has turned to green. Dirt has sprouted into growth.

It is almost as if the world adorns itself with a new set of clothes, and it's beautiful. Seeds and roots which seemed to be dead, bring life and burst forth out of the soil. This is a reminder for us and an illustration of what we see here in verses 22 through 24 of putting on new life and putting off the old man.

The effects of that around us, much like the experience that we have in spring, is that it brings life and energy. When I was studying these verses, this is the part where I became fascinated. When you are studying Scripture, it is really important to pay close attention to the verbs.

There are three verbs given here in verses 22, 23 and 24 that really help us understand the idea, and the tenses of these verbs really help us understand what is being communicated.

Let me help you see what I saw when I studied this, and maybe you will have the same wow-moment that I had. Here is the first one:

In verse 22, we see the verb "put off", and this is in an active tense. It denotes a once-and-for-all definitive action. The stripping off of my old self is to be done once and for all. This happens at the moment of this great soul-level exchange. 2 Corinthians 5 says, "Of new life we come. The old is gone." This is that putting-off moment. It happens one time.

The second verb in verse 23 is this idea of being renewed. This renewal is in a tense that implies a perpetual, cannot-be-concluded sense. I put off once and for all; I am renewed in an ongoing, active sense. Progressively, I am being renewed every single day.

And then the third verb is, I put on something, just like we read in Colossians 3:9-10. This final step of putting on is again in the same tense as that putting off; it is a one-time act. This happens at that moment of salvation. I put off the old, and I put on the new. But in the middle, there is this daily renewal that happens.

All of these verbs, this trifecta of beauty, hinges on what we read in verse 21. We see the idea, "You have been taught this; you have learned this in Christ."

Okay. Let me put all of that together. It could almost be said, "You have been taught to put off, to become new, and to put on." This is beautiful, because it really helps us understand the transformation that has happened in our lives and in the daily pursuit.

Let me reframe this in the form of an object lesson that many of you will grasp. Let's use the imagery of a garden. Instead of using the language of *put off, renew, and put on,* we'll use three other words from this imagery of a garden to help us grasp what this means.

Break

The first one is to break. Recently, I broke ground on a new garden. I've been gardening for years, and this time I took on a little bit of a different challenge because in the past, I've kind of cheated. I use raised beds, bagged soil and starter plants.

This year, for the first time ever, I'm going old school. It's virgin soil, red Georgia clay, and I'm breaking it up for the first time. The dream is that I can see what could eventually become a life-giving garden. But it means initially in this one-time act, I have to break this garden up.

This is the idea in verse 22, the initial challenge to put off the old, trust in Jesus and be made new. And when I put my trust in Jesus, I am a new creation, like we read in 2 Corinthians 15. It doesn't dissolve the reality, though, that I continue to live in a sinful world, surrounded by temptation.

Tend

Therefore, what do I have to do? I have to tend it. I have to manage it. If you have ever worked in a garden, you know that it is just that... work. Why? It is because I may have done all of this initial effort to break up the ground and get it started, but the tending or working is constant because weeds are growing. The care is daily, and the labor is backbreaking.

But between the challenge to put off and put on, Paul inserts this continual command to renew, and he acknowledges there is a spirit-level commitment, which is influenced by the Holy Spirit in our life to press on, to work out, and to strive for holiness, for the prize of the high calling of God in Christ Jesus.

Renewal is not the same as repairing. If we were to move from gardening to construction, we are not talking about caulking and sanding; we are talking about a complete demo and rebuilding. 2 Corinthians 4:16 speaks of a day-to-day, every day renewal of the inner man.

There is another passage of Scripture that is strikingly similar. Hopefully, it has even come to your mind as we have been talking about this. Romans 12:1-2 tells us:

Romans 12:1-2

I appeal to you therefore, brothers, by the mercies of God, to present your bodies as a living sacrifice, holy and acceptable to God, which is your spiritual worship. Do not be conformed to this world, but be transformed by the renewal of your mind. That by testing, you may discern what is the will of God, what is good and acceptable and perfect.

Being renewed in Christ is a daily and repeated commitment in my labor to pursue the heart of Christ. It is the core, the heart, the soul of man, often described in Scripture like in 2 Corinthians 4:16. And it requires this total, ongoing renewal.

Here is a question I'd love for you to internalize: What does daily renewal look like in your life? How does it impact your habits? How does it impact your routine? How does it impact your discipline? For me, it looks like a daily commitment in my prayer to acknowledge God's authority every morning. "God, I acknowledge your authority today. And I declare that you are God of my life today." It is a daily renewal.

Yes, there was that one-time putting off and putting on. But I daily need to remind myself. Daily I need to declare submission to His authority. Daily, I need to cry out for victory over addiction or over sin in my life.

Produce

This tending ultimately leads to productivity or producing. Anybody who goes through the work of breaking ground on a garden and tending it is going through this process. Why? I have my eye fixed on the prize of a tomato sandwich! There is not much better in the world than two pieces of plain white bread, a big slice of tomato and some mayonnaise, salt, and pepper at the end of the summer to say, "This was all worth it."

Realize that there is a prize to stretch for. I know it's shallow. I am not comparing spiritual growth and pursuit to a tomato sandwich. There is no perfect symbolism. But putting off comes before putting on. It is because we have already put off our old nature in that decisive act of repentance and conversion, that we can logically be commanded to put away all the practices that go with it, like we have just read about in Ephesians 4.

I am not hiding my sin and covering it up with goodness. It is a *change* that has taken place in me. I am a new man. I have put on this new creation in Christ as we see in verse 24. This speaks to identity. It speaks to loyalty. As we identify with Him, we work to conform to His nature, to be like Him, to love like Him, to mirror His thoughts, to think His thoughts. We have been made in His image, and we are reminded here in verse 24 to strive to be just like Him.

And then the last words here in verse 24 bring us all back to the heart of the matter of truth, as opposed to the deceit that we see in verse 22. We are to strive to be like Him, to pursue righteousness and holiness of truth and to stand on solid ground.

Anything that is alive will change. Anything that is growing will change. And a changing church will be a forged and united church, if we are all working to put on the new self and look more like Jesus. When we do, the ideas that separate us begin to blur, when we all begin to look more like our Father.

When society begins to polarize us, keep your eyes fixed on Jesus. Allow His mission to be supreme in your life. As we are renewing and following in rhythm with the Spirit, we begin to produce similar fruit, and it will be evident to the world that we are all cared for by the same master gardener, who has forged us as one.

What we will begin to see is our hope has been restored in Christ alone. We are forged as a unified church, committed more than ever to carrying hope to the world. Just like your garden requires daily attention, our faith requires a daily pursuit of Christ. For me, this involves daily recognition of authority over all the areas of my life. It influences me to acknowledge my weaknesses, desire to know Him more and strive to please Him.

Take a moment, and honestly evaluate your personal pursuit of your relationship with Jesus. Does it resemble a weed-infested garden that has laid barren for a couple of years? If so, let's get to work and pull those weeds out. Confess those things, and get back into that tending attitude of pursuit.

Or maybe it resembles a growing ground that is producing fruit. What I want us to be encouraged by as we commit to put on Christ and produce the fruit of righteousness, is a collective Church of God that more resembles His image, His nature, His thoughts and His mission.

A forged church is a unified church walking in rhythm with the Spirit of God and choosing not to walk in the cadence and the rhythm of the world.

Deep Dive

1. Ephesians 4:17-19 describes a culture that puts self first and feeds sinful desires. How can we live a holy life in a world that celebrates sin?

   _____

   _____

   _____

2. In Ephesians 4:20-21, Paul assumes that readers have put their trust in Christ. Don't assume this of your friends. Share your faith story with others, and encourage them to share their faith story with you.

3. Ephesians 4:22-24 describes the importance of daily renewal. Describe your daily spiritual discipline, and think about whose personal accountability could be beneficial.

   _____

   _____

   _____

Chapter Five

BUILDING TOGETHER

D o you enjoy watching the news? Most people don't, because most often it is filled with only negative stories. But, in the midst of the darkest of news, if we look closely, we can see inspirational moments of hope. This is helpful for us in days of confusion, anger and separation. On one hand, we see that we are a divided country. On the other hand, we can see that there can be unity within the church that can demonstrate peace, hope and love.

In the midst of darkness, disunity and pain, there are these glimmers and images of hope and encouragement. We can often see those if we are willing to cut through the noise and look hard enough. It is the response of Jesus' Church, you and me, that can cut through division.

As we look at Ephesians 4:25-32, following several verses that contain warning signs of sin, Paul is going to contrast each of them with an encouraging challenge to focus on words of truth, sharing, kindness and forgiveness. God called you and me to step out of darkness and into His glorious light in 1 Peter 2:9.

That reality should cause you and me to reframe our focus and our view of others and drive us to be forged as the people of

God to walk in unity for the sake of the truth, the security of the Spirit and for the cause of Jesus Christ.

Recommit to the Team

First, we see the importance of recommitting to the team. Let's read Ephesians 4:25.

Ephesians 4:25

Therefore, having put away falsehood, let each one of you speak the truth with his neighbor, for we are members one of another.

What does it mean to recommit to the team? A few years back, I had the privilege of serving as an administrator at Calvary Christian School. During that season, I was actually "dual-purposing", and one of my responsibilities was as the high school principal. I remember counseling a student in my office one day.

This was his first year. He was new to the school and was really struggling to connect and feel like he was a part of the school community. It was toward the end of the first semester, and I remember trying to encourage him and coach him up a little bit.

He was constantly comparing Calvary to his old school and would say, "Why do you all do this?" He would go on and on, and I remember coaching him, saying, "Here's the deal, Brother. Let me help you out. Until 'you all' becomes 'we' you are going to have a hard time connecting. When 'you all' becomes 'we', you will see and feel yourself committed to the team."

Paul has spent so much time in Ephesians 4 challenging believers to put off the old man, to walk in rhythm with the Spirit and to commit, to put on the new man. This flows out of the first seven or eight verses, this unity that we find in one God, one baptism and one glorious hope.

Here in verse 25, he continues building off of this thought with a powerful verb that makes the assumption that you have already put away falsehood. I am going to make an assumption that you have already done that. In other words, I am making an assumption that you have put off the old man, and you are committed to the team. I am making an assumption that your mindset is "we" and not "you all". This assumption implies a separation from falsehood and an identity with the truth, which becomes a plumb line.

The Bible uses this word *falsehood*, and let's just be honest; that is not a word that we use in our everyday vocabulary this way. What is falsehood anyway?

You likely immediately think of telling a lie, and that is an important consideration. I mean, a lie is a breach of a social contract that we make. It tends to make unity impossible. Unity only exists through the trust that one man puts in another man to tell the truth. A lie can turn an instrument of communication and speech, which God has given us for comfort, into an entrapment or entanglement.

Therefore, Proverbs 13:5 would tell us that a righteous man hates lying. So, falsehood certainly involves lying or not telling the truth. Certainly you see this evidence in how it impacts your marriage, parenting, working relationships and your ability to connect with your neighbor.

Falsehood is much more comprehensive than just lying, though, because it also involves holding on to the "old man" and *living* a lie. In other words, falsehood includes carrying a dark secret and pretending everything is fine. I really want to challenge you to press into this, because you may feel like, "I generally tell people the truth." That's great, but that is not fully inclusive of the idea of falsehood.

Maybe you also should ask the honest question: What are some secret sins that are a burden you are carrying all alone? How can the body of Christ promote biblical unity in sharing and carrying the weight of that? It is a life of repentance over personal sin and accountability with others in the body of believers that is a way of embracing what is true. This commitment to the team requires a commitment to the truth.

Furthermore, truth penetrates all the way to the very nature of God. So the commitment of the team requires a commitment to the truth and therefore, a commitment to the nature of God.

Truthfulness promotes unity. Truthfulness brings us together and forges us as one. Lying, on the other hand, destroys it. Ephesians is not providing some revelation that the readers have never known. I mean, we have known and clung to the idea of truth for decades, for centuries, for generations.

A love for truth manifests itself in some specific circumstances, in common conversation with people, in you giving a report about something that you have seen, in making a promise and actually keeping it, and in putting away falsehood. We live with integrity, honesty and repentance of sin. The word of a Christian ought to be his or her bond.

The Hebrew concept of truth embraces faithfulness and right-eousness. To speak the truth includes the responsibility to be a witness to truth. Follow the example of Christ to show unselfish love, build up one another and be your best. Even beyond all of that, Jesus Himself embodies truth. He defines Himself as truth in John 14:6. We as individuals, as a body of believers, are connected to the source of the spring of truth, Jesus Himself, and goodness and mercy should flow out of that.

The lynch pin here that we see in verse 25 is the idea of truth. As we walk through the following verses and points, see how they all are going to point back to the upholding of truth.

Revolt Against the Norm

We have to revolt against the norm. Now, I don't know what kind of TV shows you like to watch. Personally, I enjoy nature shows. I enjoy *National Geographic* or *The Discovery Channel*. I enjoy watching those and getting an understanding of nature and animals. One thing I am always fascinated to watch is when they show salmon spawning and swimming upstream. It is just fascinating that these creatures can do that. They flow against the current and are motivated by the innate need to reproduce.

Well, I think that is a beautiful picture of nature that illustrates an ability for you and me to notice what is a normal pattern, or stream, of culture. We should be intentional to swim upstream and revolt against what the norm is, if the norm is leading us away from how God has called us to live.

Paul is going to build on this idea of individual behavior and its impact on unity. Consider the following in verses 26 and 27:

Ephesians 4:26-27

Be angry and do not sin; do not let the sun go down on your anger, 27 and give no opportunity to the devil.

Resolve Anger

We have got to go against the norm of how culture says we should deal with anger. Oftentimes we may notice a reaction to a situation that is like a dangerous, recoiling snake of emotion. We are striking out as we react; we recoil, feeling threatened, and we react to it in anger.

There are some situations in which that response is expected. I think some of the responses we see in the world today are somewhat understandable. The big question comes in how that emotion can be applied and how it can be processed in a healthy way that does not lead to sin.

See, there have been many, many misunderstandings around the idea of anger. People say, "The Good Book says don't get angry." Well, while the Bible certainly says a lot about anger and certainly speaks to the damage it can cause, we really need to pay attention to what it says, because there are examples in Scripture of righteous anger.

Psalm 7:11 would be one where God Himself demonstrates anger. Mark 3:5 would be an example where Jesus shows anger. There are other examples in Scripture where God appears to approve of human anger. Read these verses later: Numbers 25:11, 1 Samuel 28:18, 1 Kings 22:22.

Anger is natural, and at times anger is right. Like God, we should hate and be angry when we see injustice. We should hate and show anger toward prejudice, idolatry and sin in the world and sin in our life. That hate for unrighteousness is a response of our love for the truth and what is right. But, this is the guard that we see here in Scripture: Anger may begin as a righteous response, but it can turn to sin if we allow it to root in resentment, hatred and unforgiveness.

In fact, if I am honest, most often when I experience anger generally in my life, it is due to me being selfish and prideful about something. I get angry when I don't get my way or when something didn't pan out how I preferred it to pan out. Generally for me, anger is evident not over something righteous, but over me being selfish. If we are being honest, most of the time, anger is sin.

We have got to recognize, though, that there is righteous anger, like hating and being angry toward injustice. That is good. Being angry and hating things like racism is good because it is counter to what is true. We have to pay careful attention to the text because here, there is the idea that, when you are angry, do not sin. Do not be led into sin. What starts off with proper motive can quickly turn into sin. If unchecked, that anger may destroy our peace. It may distract us from our mission.

Literally, it can paralyze and cripple us, and it can spread as a cancer to unity in the church. Verse 27 mentions that we can even give a foothold to the devil to gain traction in his attempt to thwart the advancement of God's kingdom.

What do we do? I think there are two practical safeguards here that are mentioned in God's Word that we can pay attention to. The first one is, set a time limit on your anger, making the assumption that it is a righteous thing to be angry about. Don't let the sun go down on it. Set a time limit on it, and prevent the strengthening of your anger.

Otherwise, if we don't, we will give place to the devil. What does that mean? To give place to the devil literally means to get out of the way and allow it to freely reign. The danger of giving place to the devil is primarily directed against the church's unity and against our fellowship.

Sleeping on anger causes it to grow, and selfishness sets in. It even leads to thoughts of revenge. A mere personal slight is not a cause for anger, especially when we remember Him who was led as a lamb to the slaughter. As a sheep before its shearers is silent, so He opened not His mouth (Isaiah 53:7).

Rather, we are to reserve our anger for what hurts the truth, the Gospel, what hurts the truth in us and the truth in others. This all links back to the truth that we see elevated in verse 25 in the nature of God.

Earn to Share

The second way that we can revolt against the norm is to earn to share. Let's read verse 28.

Ephesians 4:28

Let the thief no longer steal, but rather let him labor, do-
ing honest work with his own hands, so that he may have
something to share with anyone in need.

Now, I'm going to confess to you a time in my life when I learned that stealing was wrong. Correction: when I even learned what stealing *was*. I was a small boy. I had to be three and four years of age.

My dad worked in a grocery store, and I was in the store with him. We were in the checkout line. Just like now, back then, as you stood in front of the register, to your left and right were racks of candy. Dad was checking out, paying for whatever he was buying that day. I looked at what was perfect eye-level for my age, and I just grabbed some candy and put it in my pocket. I didn't think anything about it.

We walked out and got into the car. I was sitting in the passenger seat of the car as a little guy, and dad cranked it up. We were still in the parking lot, and I reached in my pocket, pulling out this piece of candy. I just start eating it. My dad says, "Son, where did you get that candy?" I said, "I got it out of the store." He puts the car in park and says, "It's time for you to come out with me."

He walks me right back through that line. Thankfully, it was a cashier he knew. (It's funny how even as small as I was, this is locked in my memory.) He walks up to the lady and says, "My son just stole something from your store, and he would like to pay you for it." Before that day, I did not understand the concept of taking something that didn't belong to me.

Now stealing, taking something that doesn't belong to you, is a disruptive force. It results in the creation of chaos. It makes unity and fellowship impossible. But we are not talking here in this text about somebody walking into a store to rob it. In the context of verse 28, this is much more than stealing a piece of candy.

Some of us, when we think about what this can mean, maybe there is a lot more stealing going on in our heart than we realize. For example, this even applies to the supplier who shortens the order and overcharges for his product. That is a thief. This applies to the employee who doesn't work faithfully to his manager's expectations for the amount of hours he is getting paid for and the duties for which he is being paid. That is stealing.

This is the doctor who drags out a visit to his patient beyond what is necessary so that he can overbill that time. That is stealing. This is the government official who taxes the people so much more than is necessary so he can pay himself an enormous salary. That is stealing. Paul says here, "Let him who stole steal no more."

If you steal the time of a diligent man, you rob him, and you rob the world, too, of that benefit. This applies to the ancient culture of the Ephesians. This applies all the way back to Homer in 850 BC. This applies to the ancient Spartan culture where they taught their boys to steal, and it was only disgraceful if they were caught. This really cuts through the heart of a lack of integrity, and it is called out as wrong. It fractures the desire for us to be forged.

In contrast, as we see in the Scripture, we are called to work hard, and this denotes useful work and useful employment that benefits others, the community. The call here is to honor others and help because we value honesty. This links all the way back to verse 25 and the concept of truth.

Rather than taking and hiding, the motive is to strengthen community. Honest labor is needful if the needy are to live. And don't read into what the text is *not* saying. This is not saying there is anything wrong with working hard and reaping the benefits of it. This is talking about being honest and working hard and helping. Why? It points back to truth.

Speak Hope to All who Hear

The third way to revolt against the norm is, we speak hope to all who hear. The words that we say have power. Let's read verses 29 and 30:

Ephesians 4:29-30

Let no corrupting talk come out of your mouths, but only such as is good for building up, as fits the occasion, that it may give grace to those who hear. And do not grieve the Holy Spirit of God, by whom you were sealed for the day of redemption.

The word used for *corrupt* here, as in corrupt talk, literally would be the same word used to describe the food on your counter that is not fresh, and is beginning to rot. Have you ever done that? You take that thing out of the fridge or off of the counter, and you give it the smell test to see if it's still okay to eat? Why? It's because it may be becoming corrupt. It started off as good, and it could be good, but it could also kill you and make you sick.

This is more than just curse words and bad language. This is speaking to the point of malicious gossip and slander and whatever injures another and feeds dissension. Our words, my words have the power to be a contagion of sin, like a virus that can spread, and it results in disunity. It can corrupt and infect the minds and the hearts of other people.

In contrast, we are encouraged to allow our speech to be an overflow of the presence of the Holy Spirit, who influences each of us every day. If we are doing that, the fruit of the Spirit, which is wholesome, healthy, and beneficial, begins to overflow with love, joy, peace, patience, gentleness, and on and on through the list in Galatians 5.

As a faith family, the ultimate source of all blessing is God Himself, and the channel He is using here is humanity. He is using us as His church in everyday conversations, believers becoming a means of grace to others. Recognition and reverence for the Holy Spirit working in our lives is the motive for enjoying profitable speech.

Nothing can be more disrespectful to God than a witness who gives rotten speech coming out of the same mouth that was given the benefit of grace. James reminds us of this when he says, "Out of the same mouth comes a blessing and cursing." He even goes on to describe the importance of taming or controlling the tongue.

I would go so far as to say this doesn't just apply to the actual spoken word, but the video recorded word, the texted word, the posted word, and the written word. What we see here is, if we allow our speech, our words, to literally rot like the vegetable on your counter, we grieve the Holy Spirit. In other words, what that means is, we disappoint Him. He is saddened by it. We break His heart.

To grieve the Holy Spirit is to help obliterate the seal and weaken the evidence of our redemption. Rather than disappoint Him by our lack of self-control in what we say, recognize Him, honor His presence and the reality of the seal of security He has marked on your life.

When we have an object that we own, we will put our mark on it. We may put our name on it to show that it's ours. A farmer who has cattle may brand his name so that if one is ever taken, people know who it belongs to.

This term that we have been sealed or branded by the Spirit of God implies identity. It implies security. It is an act of saying, "You have been sealed; you belong to Jesus." And this preserves in grace my security for eternity. I am kept and preserved by His power forever, and it lasts beyond death until the day of redemption. That seal is set for eternity.

Charles Spurgeon said, "Grieve not, then, that Spirit upon whom you are so dependent. He is your credential as a Christian. He is your life as a believer."[6]

My grieving or disappointing the Spirit doesn't break the seal, but it certainly breaks His heart. Thus, there is a connection of our seal, our identity to our unity and being forged together.

Reflect His Glory in Your Goodness

We see in verses 31 and 32, the idea that we reflect His glory in your goodness.

Ephesians 4:31-32

Let all bitterness and wrath and anger and clamor and slander be put away from you, along with all malice. Be kind to one another, tenderhearted, forgiving one another, as God in Christ forgave you.

In the first chapter, we talked about four stones referenced to anchoring points for unity, and this now is a summary concept, which includes varying kinds of wickedness that have been expressed over our study. We are challenged to put off for good the temptations that lead us to wickedness and embrace the goodness of God and allow it to influence our choices and our conduct.

There is an old movie from the year 2000, which is still a great visual of what this can look like. It was the movie, *Pay It Forward* starring Haley Joel Osment.[7] This was the idea of acts of kindness and how they are contagious and replicated in others. When someone receives kindness, they want to pay it forward and share and express that kindness to others.

With that idea in mind, we see in the text the glory and goodness of God that should be demonstrated in the kindness we express, and it is often contagious. All of our actions that have been encouraged throughout Ephesians 4 were elevating the glory of

God, drawing people together and pointing others to Him. In fact, I would say this leads us to this entire chapter in this one sentence:

The glory of God on display elevates the Gospel.

The glory of God on display in your speech, in your conduct and your love expressed to others elevates the Gospel. The kindness of some is like an echo; it returns exactly the counterpart of what is received. This isn't just my idea. It is reinforced in Matthew 5:46-47. The strength of this and its impact on being forged together is that kindness breeds kindness.

Putting off the old man encourages others to do the same. Walking in rhythm with the Spirit and the new man encourages others to do the same. One person who looks like Jesus challenges other people to want to look like Jesus. Specifically here in verse 31, we see three things that God tells us to be.

Kind

One is kind. Kindness is this feeling of affection that results in action, and the Greek language here involves serving. When you are kind and serve other people, you are demonstrating and elevating the Gospel.

Tenderhearted

He uses the language of tenderhearted. This is the idea of being impressionable, which is reflected in our thoughts. This implies a willingness to listen and understand, to observe and be sensitive to the needs of others and not be selfish in our own right and intentions.

Forgiving

Kindness, tenderheartedness and forgiveness. Forgiveness is that loving spirit which prefers to suffer rather than pain others. It sees no fault in another because it is so conscious of its own faults. It is important to notice that tenderhearted is placed in between kind and forgiving.

It is the softness of my heart that impacts my behavior, my willingness to be led by the Spirit and my ability to see the needs around me. The softness of your heart can be impacted by reflection. The softness of your heart increases the elevation of the Gospel in your actions.

Listen, no matter the extent of your sin, no matter the degree of wickedness, no matter your unjust anger, no matter your theft, no matter your rotten speech, no matter your secret sin, you are forgiven by the blood of Jesus as His child. You are kept secure by the seal of the Spirit of God as His child. Take a minute, and rest in that. Celebrate that.

God does not forgive by pressure. God forgives freely. God forgives abundantly, and He challenges you and me to do the same thing. Matthew 18:21-22 says:

Matthew 18:21-22

Then Peter came up and said to him, "Lord, how often will my brother sin against me, and I forgive him? As many as seven times?" Jesus said to him, "I do not say to you seven times, but seventy-seven times seven."

I must be willing to share what I did not deserve to receive in the first place. Forgiven people should forgive people. God, for Christ's sake, has forgiven you. Forgiven people should forgive people.

Pardon and forgiveness are not prizes to be run for, but blessings received as the first step of the race, and this forgiveness is continual, free, full and eternal. God will never bring up your past offenses and charge you for them a second time. They are forgiven, and you and I should extend that same grace to other people.

Imagine the change in our actions, in our conduct, in our behavior when we rest in our security in the Spirit, because we have trusted in the forgiveness of Christ. We have allowed Him to lead us, to walk with a faith family that values kindness and values love over selfishness and pride.

A forged, unified body of believers that holds tightly to the truth is willing to share with others. It is a safe place to experience forgiveness. This is a forged and unified people that is committed to elevate God and His Word over self. This is who we are. This is who we strive to be: forged and unified in purpose.

Deep Dive

1. Ephesians 4:25 describes a value of being part of a team. Share why being a member of a church is important to you and how your church has encouraged your walk with Christ.

   _____

   _____

   _____

2. Ephesians 4:26-30 challenges specific areas of our conduct. How does our speech, selfishness, and unresolved anger negatively impact unity in our faith family?

   _____

   _____

   _____

3. Ephesians 4:31-32 speaks to the forgiveness of Christ and how it impacts our fellowship. How should a forgiven soul be willing to offer forgiveness to others, and why is this sometimes difficult to do?

_____

_____

_____

SUMMARY

My prayer is that this book will help you grow.

The first chapter was focused on our identity in Christ and how we are called to stand out. When we are fractured, it impacts how those outside the Church view us, and it brings dishonor to the name of Jesus. What we do with our call as believers not only affects us, but it affects those around us.

Remember the stones of unity we talked about? When humility, gentleness, patience and love all come together, it is a force to be reckoned with and those characteristics bond us together.

In Chapter 2, we talked about how it is easy for the Church to become fractured over spiritual gifts and perhaps become jealous of the gifts other believers have. But this is a wrong focus. We should focus more on the *giver* of the gifts and recognize His (Jesus') authority to give as he sees best. All gifts work together for one mission, and none function well alone.

We also talked about ways to measure growth and maturity. It is important to be able to see if we are growing in maturity or not. We will not see full maturity until after this life, but we can and should make progress, particularly in our knowledge of Christ.

Chapter 3 was all about stages of growth. I described delayed growth, coordinated growth, and exponential growth, with a special emphasis on truth. Truth, personified in Jesus, is the essential core element to the unity of the Church.

Next, in Chapter 4, I contrasted the way we are to live (making a big deal out of Jesus) with the rhythm of the world around us. The rhythm of this world leads to emptiness, darkness, being excluded and having a calloused heart. As people go through that progression, they get harder and harder to the Gospel. That is why it is important to anchor our thoughts on Jesus and not on the culture around us.

Finally, Chapter 5 was about seeing the Church as "we" rather than "you all" or "them". We are a team, and we work out problems together. The world is often marked by falsehood and anger, but we should be marked by a radical love of truth, kindness and forgiveness.

We can be forged together in unity if we are all committed to the same goal of growing in Jesus for the sake of His Kingdom. Remember our high, holy calling. Treat each other with love, working against the things that divide us. And keep your eyes on the Truth. Like you, I am a work in progress, but hopefully this book will help us get a little bit closer to unity, both in the local church and the Church universal.

REFERENCES

[1]*Avengers: Endgame* [Motion picture]. (2019). S.l.: Marvel.

[2]Chapman, G. D. (2010). The five love languages: How to express heartfelt commitment to your mate. Bhopal, India: Manjul Pub.

[3]Barrows, Cliff, and Don Hustad. Crusader Hymns: for Church, School and Home. Hope Publishing Co., 1966.

[4]"ESPN Documentary 'The Last Dance' About Michael Jordan and the Chicago Bulls, Gets a New Trailer". Maxim. December 24, 2019. Archived from the original on December 28, 2019. Retrieved May 2020.

[5]Maxwell, J. C. (2008). The 21 irrefutable laws of leadership. Nashville, TN: Thomas Nelson.

[6]The Spurgeon Center. (1867, March 03). Retrieved September 24, 2020, from https://www.spurgeon.org/resource-library/sermons/grieve-not-the-holy-spirit/

[7]Leder, M. (Director). (2001). *Pay it forward* [Video file]. Burbank, CA.: Warner Home Video. Retrieved May 2020, from https://www.imdb.com/title/tt0223897/

Barth, M. (2008). Ephesians: Introduction, translation, and commentary on chapters 4-6 (Vol. 34A, p. 441). New Haven; London: Yale University Press.

Best, E. (1998). A critical and exegetical commentary on Ephesians (p. 404). Edinburgh: T&T Clark International.

Exell, J. S. (n.d.). *The Biblical Illustrator: Ephesians* (pp. 392–393). New York; Chicago; Toronto; London; Edinburgh: Fleming H. Revell Company.

Graham, G. (2008). *An Exegetical Summary of Ephesians* (2nd ed., p. 322). Dallas, TX: SIL International.

The Holy Bible: English Standard Version. (2016). (Eph 4:14–16). Wheaton, IL: Crossway Bibles.

Slater, T. B. (2012). *Ephesians.* (R. A. Culpepper, Ed.) (p. 118). Macon, GA: Smyth & Helwys Publishing, Inc.

Spence-Jones, H. D. M. (Ed.). (1909). *Ephesians* (p. 150). London; New York: Funk & Wagnalls Company.

Stott, J. R. W. (1979). *God's new society: the message of Ephesians* (p. 172). Downers Grove, IL: InterVarsity Press.

ABOUT THE AUTHOR

Pastor Ricky Smith is currently the lead pastor of Calvary Baptist Church in Columbus, Georgia and provides leadership to the multi-faceted ministry with a commitment to make disciples in the Chattahoochee Valley and to the ends of the earth. Ricky's ministry career has been focused on making the name of Jesus known and advancing the mission of the Gospel.

He received a bachelor's degree in Christian Education with an emphasis in Youth Ministry from Bryan College. He holds a Masters degree in Theology from Liberty Baptist Seminary, and he holds a Specialist Degree in Educational Leadership from Liberty University. He also holds an honorary doctorate from Emmanuel Theological Seminary.

Follow Ricky on social media using @rickylamarsmith.

www.ingramcontent.com/pod-product-compliance
Lightning Source LLC
Chambersburg PA
CBHW070814050426
42452CB00011B/2038